Horse Whispers & Lies

To Larry & Laura —

Because Truth does Matter!

Nice chatting with you in Reno, NV.

Enjoy

Deborah An Ristau

Joyce Rensboone

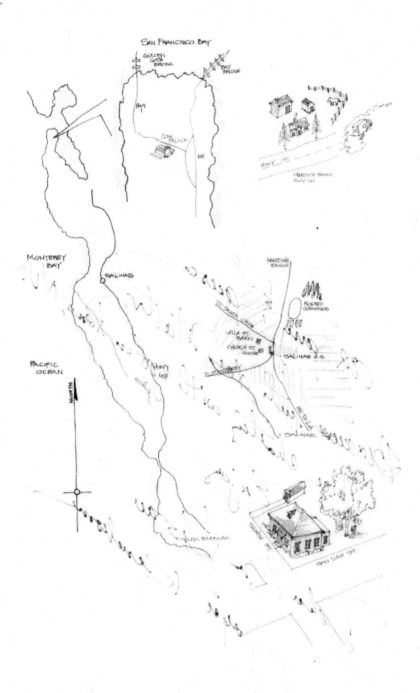

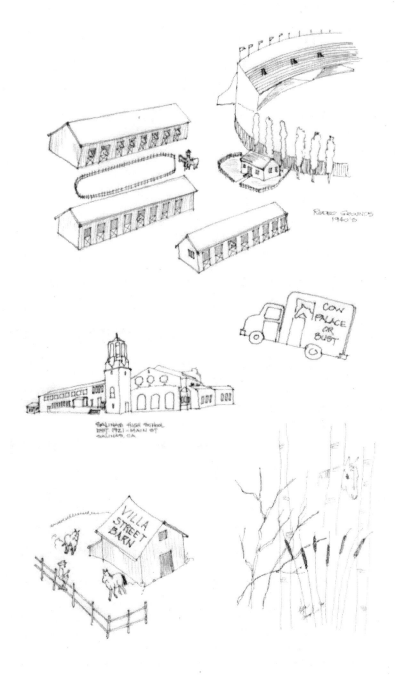

Horse Whispers & Lies

Debra Ann Ristau
&
Joyce Martins Renebome

1999
Veracity Books
Berkeley, California

Horse Whispers & Lies

Editor: Roy M. Carlisle
Copyeditor: Karyn S. DiCastri
Cover: Julie Orona, Never Boring Design
Illustrations: Vern Fergel
Author Photo: Steve Strohm
Printed in the United States of America
All photographs are courtesy of authors
unless otherwise noted.

ISBN 1-929055-44-7
Library of Congress Catalog Card Number:
99-95062
Printed in the United States of America

Veracity Books
Berkeley, California

http://www.horsewhispersandlies.com

To Marvin and Marguerite,
until we ride together again . . .

Junior riders with Marguerite Roberts at the rodeo grounds, Salinas, CA, circa 1948.

Front Row, Left to right: *Jim Barker, Ron Stolich, John Meyenberg, Joyce Martins, Larry Roberts, John Ingram, Diane Laporte, Marguerite Roberts.*

Second Row, l to r: *Bill Sprague, Dick Gillott, Sandra Stolich, Jim Laporte, LaVerne Hearn.*

Third Row, l to r: *Mike McPharlin, unknown, Shirley Hager, Monty Roberts, Tom Parker, John Fiscalini, Barbara Harris, Joanne Swensen, Jimmie Krieger.*

Sincere Appreciation

To our wonderful husbands, Dave and Pete; we cannot express enough love and gratitude for the sacrifices they made. Their love and understanding bolstered our determination. They gave us moral support—or a shoulder to cry on—when the odds seemed insurmountable.

Our loving appreciation goes to Larry Roberts and his wife, Jamie. Larry's prodigious files, memorabilia, and hours of tearful interviews were invaluable in our search to document the truth.

Supporting our determination to celebrate the lives of Marvin and Marguerite, and helping in so many ways, warm and loving thanks to *all* members of the Martins and Roberts families. Most especially to Lou, Lois, Jim, Sally, Beek, Kay, Bud, Merce, Hart, Lillian, Carolyn, Lynn, Curtis, Cheri, Crystal, Marguerite, Josh, Heidi, Marti, Ray, Larry, Carol and Steve.

We also wish to pay special recognition to Alan Balch, Andrée Forzani, Angie Garcia, Peggy Goemens, Skeeter Innocenti, Joanne Johnson, Cynthia Kennedy, Ann Komick, Chet Moore, Ron Stolich, and Caroline Tugle. Their faith, encouragement, and empathy were blessings we cherish.

Sincere gratitude to brave journalists and their publications that investigated and helped tell our story: Kathy Boccella, *Philadelphia Enquirer*; Eric Brazil, *San Francisco Examiner*; Doreen Carvajal, *New York Times*, Ronna Snyder, *Horse and Rider*; and James Willwerth, *Time Magazine*. Each dared to listen for the truth.

We also appreciate the editors and publishers of *Ropers Sports News* who were compelled to print several passionate letters from the family and also from Monty. A very special note of thanks goes to James Willwerth who suggested the title, *Horse Whispers & Lies.*

These backstage assistants helped make *Horse Whispers & Lies* a record of truth.

The California Rodeo Association
The John Steinbeck Public Library, Salinas, CA
The Monterey County Historical Society
The Monterey County Sheriff's Posse
The National Steinbeck Center, Salinas, CA
Sacred Heart School, Salinas, CA
The Salinas Californian
The Salinas Police Department
The Sacramento County Public Library
Santa Barbara County Clerk Recorder
Jim and Louise Barnick
Roy M. Carlisle
Dick and Jacquie Daley
Karyn S. DiCastri
Vern Fergel
Never Boring Design
Jeff and Cheryl Read
Steve Strohm

With a deluge of contributors to defend the honor of Marvin and Marguerite, we let a few voices speak for the multitude. We apologize to anyone not mentioned or inadvertently omitted.

Author's Note

This work attempts to share the true history of a gentle man whose integrity and character are being maliciously castigated.

There is a quiet evolution taking place.

Horses and humans are bonding in a positive way that many thought was impossible. This gentle phenomenon has earned many titles. Some call it "natural horsemanship," others like the term coined by novelist Nicolas Evans, "horse whispering."

Whatever the name, the message is similar: humans do not have to use force, abusive treatment, or cruelty, to teach horses. In fact, much is gained, and the experience is much more rewarding, if humans would take the time to learn the language of the horse.

Long before there was talk of horse whisperers and natural horsemanship, however, gifted horsemen and women understood and used similar principals in their training programs. The concept is not as revolutionary or new to knowledgeable and respected horse handlers as it may seem, but methodologies, techniques, and nomenclatures vary among those who offer to share their knowledge and expertise.

While the be-kind message delivered by most of these clinicians is proving beneficial to the industry and to horses, it is a travesty of morality that one such crusader appears to base his fame and training methodology on lies, trickery, and the demeaning of others.

Monty Roberts makes hideously false claims that his father was a cruel, abusive, racist who beat his son and was cruel to his horses.

Feeding off these lies, journalists and others are now using the senior Roberts to exemplify the behavior of a cruel horse trainer. Marvin Roberts, dead since

1985, cannot defend his honor or the statements he made that have been taken out of context to shame him.

Moreover, the legend of Monty Roberts and how he learned the language of horses goes unchallenged. It's been said that a tale told often takes on its own reality. Monty insists that he began to learn the nonverbal method of communication he calls Equus when he studied wild mustangs as a teenager. For weeks at a time, he says, he rode the Nevada wilderness and peered through binoculars at the feral herds, studying their behavior for hours. In reality, much of his story is a tall tale peddled as nonfiction in *The Man Who Listens to Horses* (Monty Roberts, 1997).

Portions of *Horse Whispers & Lies* describe training techniques that were used by Marvin E. Roberts. This is not a horse training manual and should not be considered to be one. We hope to provide an understanding that Marvin's training methods were not only, "not thought to be cruel at the time," but that they were not cruel.

It is our sincere hope that the leaders of this gentle and sensitive evolution are not offended by anything found here. Just as their training methods differ from one another, they are sure to differ from Marvin's. These trainers are bringing an awareness to the public and to an emerging group of new horse owners.

We salute the efforts of trainers like Tom and Bill Dorrance, Ray Hunt, Buck Brannaman, John Lyons, and Pat Parelli, who continue to offer advice with quiet dignity. A character trait of gifted horse communicators.

The horse is a noble, trusting animal who deserves the very best in human companionship. A true horseman is an honorable man, an honest man, a humble man—he is not a huckster.

About *Horse Whispers & Lies*

Horse Whispers & Lies was developed from the contributions of people who were close to Monty and/or his parents, innumerable interviews, reports, observations, photographs, clippings, documents, and hours of research.

Due to the sensitive nature of *Horse Whispers & Lies,* which refutes the work of another author, we feel these contributions, along with numerous excerpts from *The Man Who Listens to Horses* are necessary for credibility and understanding. All excerpts from *The Man Who Listens to Horses* are from the Random House first edition, 1997 unless noted otherwise.

We urge readers to use Appendixes I and II, (pp. 332, 333) as a guide throughout this book.

"Fact is the underpinning of morality," said Suzannah Lessard, author of *The Architect of Desire* at the 1997 National Book Awards. "The issue came up," she said, "because there were some books where we had to wonder about the nature of the material. There were memoirs," she said, "that reconstructed extraordinarily detailed conversations from decades past. It raised an issue for us that it was an imaginary work."

Readers of nonfiction have a right to expect the truth. Anything less is false advertising—a crime in any other business. Should the book business not be held to the same standards?

Contents

1999, National Steinbeck Center, Salinas, CA

The engraved brass plate goes largely unnoticed, with only a handful of people who ask if the dedication to Marvin and Marguerite Roberts is connected to *The Man Who Listens to Horses.* Visitors are more interested in climbing aboard Jody's pony or learning to use his grooming equipment.

In 1998, the National Steinbeck Center was opened to celebrate the literary genius of John Steinbeck. His writings, with their compassionate understanding and portrayal of human life, values, and common justice, led him to receive the Pulitzer prize in 1940 and the Nobel prize for literature in 1962. It was in 1933 that he wrote *The Red Pony;* a story of lessons learned by a boy who is given the gift of a pony.

The Red Pony Stall Exhibit at the center depicts the pages of Steinbeck's novelette in life-size reality. It also honors the memories of Marvin and Marguerite Roberts who shared lessons of life and love with hundreds of children and horses in and around Steinbeck's hometown of Salinas.

The exhibit occupies only a few square yards but is the hands-on favorite of children who stop there. The small dedication plate belies the mountainous debt of gratitude on which it was created.

Prologue

A Family Is Shocked

It seemed like any other day. There was no magical sign or prophetic omen to indicate her life was soon going to change forever. Through towering eucalyptus and slatted miniblinds, the late afternoon sun filtered across the heavy oak desk.

Outside, the resonant bellow of a bull could be heard over the chattering wrens. Joyce's home-based office was perfect for her. A real estate broker who also raised pure-bred bulls with her husband, Pete, Joyce had little spare time, and she wasn't about to spend it commuting.

Joyce would be sixty-two on her next birthday. She rarely took time off from work. *Work keeps me young,* she told herself often. She was lucky to be blessed with good health, a stimulating career, Pete, and the cattle they loved.

Seems like I'm working harder as I get older. Maybe I should think about retiring. A smile came to her lips. *No, not yet. There's always a challenge . . . always something new*, she thought as the telephone rang.

"Hello, Joyce speaking," she answered in her customary manner, closing the open file on the computer to concentrate on the caller.

"Hi, Mom, I've got the video recorder set to tape Monty tonight. Eight o'clock, right?" It was her oldest daughter, forty-two-year-old Debra.

"Yes. That's when the show starts. Cheri gets it an hour earlier in Idaho. She's going to tape it too."

"Good," said Debra, adding, "I'm so excited, Mom. It's hard to believe Monty wrote a book and we didn't know about it until now! Imagine—a bestseller! I can't wait to read it!"

"I was thinking the same thing," Joyce responded. "I'll call him tomorrow and try to get copies for us," she added before hanging up. Joyce let her eyes drift for a moment to a photo of her sister's son, Monty, among those displayed on the wall in her office.

I miss Marguerite, she thought. *If Marguerite were alive, she'd have been the first to call and tell me about Monty.*

Why didn't Monty tell us? The thought was puzzling, but not worth a lot of mental energy. She had work to do. *Where does the time go?*

8:00 P.M.

Joyce heard the distinctive ring of her telephone over the blaring television announcement that *Dateline NBC* would be airing next. *That has to be Cheri,* Joyce thought as she reached for the receiver, anxious to hear what her youngest daughter thought of Monty's television interview to promote his book, *The Man Who Listens to Horses.*

"Mom?" *Strange,* thought Joyce, *it sounds like Cheri is crying.*

"Monty said . . . that Uncle Marvin . . . hit him with a chain . . . when he was only seven years old. They made it sound like Uncle Marvin . . . was some awful . . . cruel man . . . who beat horses . . . and beat Monty." Her words tumbled out between sobs and sniffles. "It was horrible . . . awful. How could he say that?" thirty-nine-year-old Cheri asked her mother.

Cheri misunderstood something, thought Joyce.

"Calm down," Joyce said slowly to her daughter who was usually so pragmatic and unemotional. "What are you talking about? Monty couldn't have said that."

"But he did!"

"Cheri, listen to me. What you are saying doesn't make sense. Marvin was always kind and gentle. He never abused Monty or anyone else, and you know as well as I do that he wasn't cruel to horses."

As she spoke to calm her daughter, Joyce's mind raced. *This cannot be happening,* she thought. *Why would Monty invent a story of abuse and cruelty? No answer made sense.* Joyce could not imagine anyone doing that to a parent and certainly not the nephew who, because they were close in age, she knew more like a brother.

I was there, she thought. *Monty's parents were like my second parents. My sister, Marguerite, was eighteen when she gave birth to Monty.*

Joyce was just six months old then. *This is ridiculous. Cheri must be wrong,* she thought.

"Just watch the show, Mom," Cheri said. "He even cries when he talks about it. I wanted to throw up. I know I never saw Uncle Marvin be cruel to any horse or person. I can't even imagine him being cruel. He was always so kind and gentle. This show is so awful mom . . . it's so unfair . . . just watch it." Cheri was beginning to get her emotions under control. "Maybe that's why he never told us about the book," she added. "Uncle Marvin is dead. He can't even defend himself against Monty's accusations. People are going to believe Monty. He is very convincing."

"What's he doing in that tweed cap?" Pete asked, as Monty appeared on the television set. "What happened to his Stetson?"

Joyce also wondered why Monty looked and sounded so different from the California cowboy she had known for more than sixty years.

"I suppose that's part of marketing. He's supposed to be a big hit with the queen of England. I wonder when he picked up the British accent?" Joyce mused.

Cheri had warned her, but the shock, outrage, and hurt Joyce felt as she watched Monty and listened to the insidious lies and accusations leveled at his father were palpable.

Sixty-one-year-old Monty Roberts claimed on national television that when he was a seven-year-old boy his father beat him with a chain because he dared to suggest that horses could be trained with kindness.

It was quite a performance. Complete with a tearful episode during which Monty excused himself from the camera to recompose.

Joyce stared in stunned silence as Pete, her husband of forty-three years, held her hand.

Abusive? Cruel? Domineering? Marvin? No one who really knew my brother-in-law could describe him with those words, Joyce thought to herself. *Who was buying these lies? Certainly not anyone familiar with the true Marvin Roberts. How did Monty think he could get away with this?*

She squeezed Pete's work-roughened hand with her own and said, "If this weren't so nauseating, I could almost laugh. It's so absurd. He has to make a retraction. This is wrong. Monty *knows* this is wrong." Joyce could not imagine how painful it would have been for Marvin to hear Monty's words.

No man could have loved horses or children more than Marvin did. I know as surely as I know my own name that there is no basis for Monty to make these accusations, Joyce thought.

She listened as Monty eloquently spoke of horses. He was saying that as a boy he spent weeks alone with wild mustangs in the high deserts of Nevada. Her jaw fell slack, and her hand, once fiercely gripping Pete's, went limp as she listened to Monty tell of his adventures in Nevada while studying wild horse behavior and how he learned the language he calls Equus. *Equus? Weeks alone with wild horses?*

"This is all more than I can stand," said Joyce. "How can anyone tell lies like that and get away with it? God only knows what's in his book."

Joyce's sister and Monty's mother, Marguerite Martins Roberts (often called "Flick" by family and friends), had been every bit as vociferous and assertive as she was kind, loving, and generous.

Heaven forbid, Flick must be turning in her grave, thought Joyce.

Try as she did to sleep that night, Joyce tossed and turned until dawn. A persistent question burned in her heart: *Doesn't the truth matter anymore?*

Marguerite & Marvin, circa 1949. (Photo courtesy of Carol Roberts Silva).

Part I

It Began with a Dream of Children & Horses

THE RED PONY

Jody never waited for the triangle to get him out of bed after the coming of the pony.

—John Steinbeck

Chapter 1

1856–1998, SALINAS, CALIFORNIA

Elias Howe's wagon was heavy with lumber as he made his way north. An enterprising individual, he surmised there was money to be made from the hordes of immigrants moving onto California soil, and he hoped to build a tavern and cater to the travelers.

The site he had selected was east of Monterey and south of San Francisco, at the north end of the long valley he now traveled. It had been an arduous journey to bring supplies, but the promise of wealth spurred Elias through the mustard weeds growing wild and tall across the valley floor.

Near to his destination, his wagon finally gave out. Overcome with fatigue and lacking the parts he needed to repair the broken wheel, Elias decided the location would suffice for his tavern. He purchased land at the intersection of the Monterey–San Juan Bautista and Los Angeles–San Franciso stage lines from Jacob Leese and built his tavern. When the tavern was complete, Elias dubbed it the "Half Way House." And on this same site, 142 years later, the National Steinbeck Center was built.

The Man Who Listens to Horses:

> The [rodeo] grounds came to exist when Eugene Sherwood died and willed to the city of Salinas 2,300 acres to be used solely for horse-related activities. (pp.36, 37)

The area thrived. In 1867, Alanson Riker, William Jackson, and a cattle rancher named Eugene Sherwood drew plans for the town that would become Salinas. Between 1868 and 1869, Salinas grew from a small complex of twelve buildings to a community of more than a hundred buildings. By 1872, Salinas was bustling with seven hundred residents.

As the city grew, Sherwood planned for parks, schools, and churches, designating land for each. He thoughtfully mapped out the city and charted for future development.

For a seventy-acre parcel north of town, he made special plans. In 1872, the Monterey County Agricultural Association built a racetrack, grandstand, stable, bar, and restaurant on the site. It became known as the Sausal Park Racetrack.

The property was given to the city with a proviso that a fair and horse races be held every two years or the title would revert to the former owners. In 1878, Sherwood was honored when the name of the park was changed to Sherwood Park. Eventually the stables, racetrack, and grandstand areas would be called the Salinas Rodeo Grounds.

More than one hundred years later it would be renamed the Salinas Sports Complex, and today the annual rodeo and horse races remain a lasting tradition. Eugene Sherwood left a notable thumbprint on the city of Salinas.

1924, SALINAS

By 1924, Salinas had become the wealthiest per capita city in the United States of America.[1] With a population of 4,304 at the onset of the Roaring Twenties, Salinas continued to attract newcomers. An abundance of jobs and financial opportunities awaited those who found

---

[1] Kent Seavey, *A Short History of Salinas.* (Salinas: Monterey County Historical Society, 1997).

their way to this growing community of farmers, ranchers, laborers, and financiers.

The history books may recall Salinas as wealthy in 1924, but the division between families with money and those that provided the backbreaking labor to till the soil and pave the roads was nearly impassable.

Salinas lies at the north end of a long valley. The Salinas Valley—lush with crops of lettuce and beans cultivated from acres and acres of rich soil.

Through the valley runs the river. The Salinas River—bringing an abundance of water for crops, livestock, and a rapidly increasing population.

Protecting the valley are the mountains. The Gabilan Mountains rise to Fremont's Peak in the east and the Santa Lucia range boasts Mount Toro on the west—all awash in wild oats and mustard, imbued with the heady scents of oak, pine, and sage.

Clustered in the city and scattered across the valley, along the river, and in the mountains, are the people who have chosen to settle here. From varied backgrounds and ethnic persuasions they came, strong and determined people—committed to honesty and hard work.

This would become the land, the city, the home, and the very existence of Marvin and Marguerite Roberts. Never considered affluent, their wealth would someday be measured by one of God's greatest treasures—the love of those who knew them. It was here in Salinas that their story began.

1924, Martins' Ranch, Salinas

It had been more than a month since the devastating fire consumed the small crop Frank Martins planted. He had a family to feed. With four children and a fifth on the way, there was precious little time to waste. He

27

and his wife, Mame, had to make a decision about their future. Without the money from the bean crop, the ranch might be lost to creditors. This was unthinkable.

Tuna and salmon were abundant off the California coast, and Frank heard talk of the growing demand for seafood. He discussed options with Mame.

Together they made a decision. Frank would return to the sea and the fishing trade of his Portuguese ancestors. Mame would stay on the farm and care for the land, livestock, and children. The arrangement was not ideal, but times were not ideal.

Salinas was their home. They would do what was necessary to keep the ranch. Despite the rigors of work, Frank, Mame, and the children were happy here. Their oldest daughter, christened Marguerite, was eight. Still very young, she was old enough to help her mother with some of the chores and help look after her three younger brothers.

Interview with Bud Martins, Marguerite's brother, 1998:

"Marguerite loved to be in charge. From the time we were small children she liked to tell me, and everyone else, what to do."

1924, CARUTHERS, CALIFORNIA

About one hundred miles inland from the Salinas Valley, east of the Gabilan Mountains and still west of the imposing Sierra Nevada's, lies California's largest valley—the great central valley—the San Joaquin. Farming and ranching communities like Salinas were sprouting everywhere in the state, including the San Joaquin Valley. One of the towns built there is known as Caruthers.

California continued to lure newcomers. Green pastures, sandy beaches, and sunny skies brought scores of immigrants in search of the good life. Though many were disappointed, fortunes were also made. Earl and Eliza Roberts didn't make a fortune. The income from their small dairy didn't go far.

As a young man, Earl had worked on a road crew for the government. The back-breaking work was not what he had dreamed of for himself, but it was an opportunity to get a paycheck and a start in life. The job also brought Eliza Parker into his life.

Eliza was a spirited woman with a modicum of Native American blood in her veins—one-sixteenth Cherokee. She married Earl when he asked for her hand and bore him five children.

The couple worked hard to provide for the needs of their family but their early dreams of making a fortune had died long ago. They were resigned to an existence on their small dairy operation and hoped it would be enough. The oldest of their children, Lester, had already left home to make it on his own. The next to go would be Marvin.

Marvin was already eighteen. He helped with the livestock and did odd jobs to help the family out, but he sensed it was time that he should head out and make it on his own.

1925, Salinas

Nineteen-year-old Marvin had heard that a man who was good with a horse could find work in Salinas. He could think of nothing he would like better than to spend his days working with horses.

Growing up, he said his best friend had been Nellie, the mare his family used to pull the buggy. Marvin often claimed with a chuckle that he used to sneak out of the house at night to spend time with her.

The Man Who Listens to Horses:

I wish I knew [my grandmother's] Indian name; they called her Sweeney, [named] after the agent who had transported her family to Nevada. Among her few possessions were papers qualifying her as a full-blooded Cherokee . . . . (p.67)

When Ray, her youngest child, was eleven years old, Sweeney decided that her marriage contract with Earl had been fulfilled. . . . [Months later] they discovered that she had walked . . . to the Cherokee Indian Reservation, a distance of 600 miles. . . . [She] spoke little English . . . (p.67)

Ray was adopted into the Cherokee tribe and raised to adulthood. . . . learning the Indian way as well as the white man's way. Uncle Ray told me [how] the Cherokee . . . capture wild horses . . . . (p.67) [Eventually] it would form the basis of my technique in working with horses. (p.68)

Interview with Ray Roberts, Marvin's brother, 1998:

"It was sometime around nineteen twenty-seven or nineteen twenty-eight that I took off one day with three other boys to go fishing. When we got home, my family was gone. They had moved. Just like that. I was on my own. I guess I was around thirteen [years old].

"I ended up staying with my friend Henry and his mother who lived on a ranch up above [the town known as] Porterville. I was lucky because I was able to finish school while I lived with them.

"There was an Indian reservation near Henry's place. When it came time for me to move on, I went there. I told them [Native Americans] that my mother was part Cherokee and they let me stay. Our mother was actually only one-sixteenth Cherokee Indian.[2] Her name was Eliza Parker and she spoke perfect English.

"Anyway, I worked for the Indians for a few years. I tended their cattle, and they gave me food and a place to sleep in return. Thankfully, I wasn't at the reservation too long before my older brother Marvin helped me find work across the mountains in Salinas.

"I was never adopted into any [Native American] tribe and I never told Monty that I was. I have no idea why he thinks that I told him how they [Cherokee Indians] capture wild horses or how they do anything else. I couldn't have.

"He's correct about my mother leaving the family, but I was older than eleven [years of age]. However, she didn't walk to any reservation six hundred miles away! She left with a salesman named [Jack] Sweeney. I guess that's why Monty used that name for her."

1930, SALINAS

By 1930, Marvin Roberts was doing what he liked to do best. Just south of the high school on Main Street, Jack Taylor had a few acres where he took in horses to

---

[2] The Official Birth Certificate of Ray Roberts lists his mother as Eliza Parker. Under "Color or Race" she is identified as *"white."*

be trained. Marvin went to work for Taylor and began to make a living riding the horses he loved so much.

While working for Taylor, Marvin met a genial fellow by the name of Bert MacIntosh who would become a lifelong friend. Bert said that it was Marvin's job to gentle the horses and turn them into riding mounts. They called it "breaking and training" in those days.

Taylor, like others, had confidence in Marvin's abilities. Bert remembered the way Marvin was unruffled and understanding around the horses. Bert said Marvin was especially patient with horses and would tell others not to push them to learn too quickly. He reported that Marvin always said the horses needed time to learn their lessons well, and only by watching Marvin closely and observing the response of his horses, was Bert able to comprehend what he meant.

Marvin loved his life in Salinas. The only thing missing was a family of his own. Someday, he told his friends, he would meet the right girl. Until then, Marvin was content to work with horses and ride at a few rodeos on the weekends.

Marvin missed his little brother Ray. When he learned that Ray was ready to find a paying job, he asked his little brother to join him in Salinas.

Interview with Ray Roberts, Marvin's brother, 1998:

"When Marvin learned that I was looking for work, he got word to me almost immediately. He was sure I could find a job in Salinas.

"I arrived in town around nineteen twenty-nine or nineteen-thirty, and spent my last fifteen cents on breakfast, then I met up with Marvin. I stayed with him for a time, and we worked to

build a riding arena in [the nearby town of] Gonzales.

"Later on, I worked for the riding school on the rodeo grounds. I even worked for the police department for a time. Eventually I landed a job at the Jeffrey Hotel, where I worked for more than twenty years. During that time, I managed to get a ranch of my own, horses, and a wonderful family. Before that, Marvin was my only real family."

1932, SALINAS

The first time Marguerite layed eyes on Marvin he was riding a horse down Main Street. A student at Salinas High School, Marguerite was a spirited sixteen-year-old who would later tell stories about seeing the man in the black cowboy hat: the man of her dreams.

SALINAS HIGH SCHOOL
EST. 1921 - MAIN ST.
SALINAS, CA.

Chapter 2

1933, Salinas

When Marvin asked Frank and Mame for Marguerite's hand in marriage, they agreed with the stipulation that Marvin become Catholic. He would have to attend classes, be baptized, receive Holy Communion, and be confirmed as a Soldier of Christ before Frank and Mame would allow their daughter to wed this man they liked so much. Marvin agreed.

1933, Sacred Heart Church, Salinas, November 6

Marguerite was only seventeen. Standing in the vestibule, she ached to be his wife. She was in love and had dreamed of this day. Her radiant smile exuded self-satisfaction and confidence as she stepped slowly toward the altar.

They made a handsome couple. She, with her dark hair, eyes, sweetheart lips, and dimple in her chin. He, tall and handsome, with a squared jaw and high forehead that gave his face a determined appearance. His deep-set eyes barely hid the twinkle of merriment behind a usually serious countenance. On this day, his grin was wide, showing a full set of even white teeth.

He had been initially taken by her beauty but was later drawn to her strength of character, boldness, and family. Yes, Marguerite possessed the qualities Marvin desired in a wife.

How he had longed for a family of his own. He was twenty-seven now. He was ready. Marvin had always loved horses and all animals, but for Marvin, it was time to start the family he could call his own. Becoming a

Catholic hadn't been so difficult. He was thankful that Marguerite's brother Bud had helped him with the studying. Marvin loved his bride's entire family and showed them with his words and actions at every opportunity.

At twenty-seven, Marvin's close-cropped brown hair was worn combed back and slightly to one side. Few people ever saw his hair. He was seldom indoors and rarely removed his characteristic cowboy hat. On this day, he dressed with care and and was meticulously groomed.

Marvin was a man slowly gaining all that he desired from life. He could not take his eyes off Marguerite as she walked down the aisle toward him. He wanted this vision to last forever so he seared the details in his mind, like a photograph he could retreive, to look upon for the rest of his life.

As Bud, whose given name is Ernest, watched his sister exchange the vows of holy matrimony with Marvin, he wondered what changes would take place at home.

The oldest sibling, Marguerite had always been bossy. *Real bossy,* Bud thought. Bud had encountered her ire more than once. He thought of how she used to help their mother with the chores and how she relished her position as the oldest child.

Bud smiled as his big sister kissed Marvin. Bud loved her and knew that she loved him in return.

The Man Who Listens to Horses:

> My mother was also a subservient soul who walked in my father's shadow.... (p.51)

Interview with Bud Martins, Marguerite's brother, 1998:

"When we were children, [Marguerite] would make this big production of work schedules for us boys while she tended to the chores outside. She worked hard like we all had to in those days. She just liked to work outdoors.

"When she didn't get her way, she could be darn hard to get along with. I remember that she used to get in trouble for being bossy. She was forever telling us what to do and how we were supposed to do it. That's just how she was.

"But she was also loving and kind and would do anything for you, especially if you couldn't do it for yourself. It's just that she never let anyone tell her what to do.

"She and Marvin lived with our family for a short time after they got married in nineteen thirty-three. I don't think she treated Marvin any different than she treated the rest of us. She sure wasn't subservient to him.

"She was sassy and loud, but she was always, always, a good person. She never changed."

1935, SALINAS

On May 14, 1935, the Roberts' first child was born. A healthy boy with his father's good looks, he possessed a broad chin with a hint of a dimple. The arrival of Marvin Jr. came just six months after Mame gave birth to Joyce, the last of the eight Martins children.

With a new baby of their own, Frank and Mame were now *grandparents* too. The family atmosphere was changing.

1936, SALINAS

Fourteen months after Marvin Jr. was born, Marguerite gave birth to their second child—another boy. They named him Larry.

By the fall of 1936, Marguerite's little sister Joyce seemed as much a part of the Roberts household as their own two boys. Marguerite often looked after Joyce while her mother was working. Watching the three babies at play, neither Marvin nor Marguerite could have predicted the future that awaited them. Nor could they have imagined the direction of their individual growth.

THE RODEO GROUNDS: A HISTORY

Monterey County historian Burton Anderson has documented much of the history of Salinas and of the California Rodeo. According to Anderson, when the Sausal Racetrack and Park was built in 1872 there was a stipulation that a fair and horse race was to be held every two years. Though popular at first, less than forty years later that popularity was sadly diminished.

In 1909, several area ranchers came together to rekindle enthusiasm for the event. They made grand plans for a huge barbecue that included copious amounts of whiskey and beef. One member, Iver "Red" Cornett, thought it would be good to have a bucking horse show fill the time between races and made arrangements with livestock dealer Frank J. Griffen.

The first show held at the park got underway on August 1, 1911, and ran for an entire week. To this day, the California Rodeo is held during what is called "Big Week" in Salinas.

The word rodeo comes from the Spanish word *rodear* meaning to roundup. *(Most American rodeos pro-*

nounce the name ro-dee-o, but the California Rodeo retains the original Spanish flavor with ro-day-o.) It was used by the Spanish rancheros to describe the spring days when cattle were gathered for branding and castration. In the fall, another rodeo was held when fattened cattle were brought in for slaughter. The semiannual roundup on the big ranchos was the precursor to modern rodeo. The event served as a social gathering for the families and could often last a week or longer. The rodeo usually included barbecues, dances, and competition among the *vaqueros.*

During that first Big Week in 1911, James R. Hebbron led a parade of one hundred riders down Salinas' Main Street, and the daily horse parade became part of the annual event. Hebbron led the parade until his ninety-seventh birthday in 1936.

In 1912, four thousand people attended the rodeo and women were included as participants. By 1923, the California Rodeo was a tradition and an embedded part of Salinas' heritage. That year, the Rodeo Association presented the city with forty-thousand-dollars to obtain a quit claim deed from the Sherwood heirs. Subsequently, a new grandstand, a racetrack, barns, and fences were built. In 1926, local service clubs sponsored a Queen of the Rodeo contest that has since evolved to the Miss California Rodeo contest, open to young women throughout the state.

By 1929, "professional" cowboys outnumbered "local" cowboys in competition and 'Rodeo' was on the brink of recognition as a viable sporting event. The daily horse parade however, was still comprised mostly of local riders and extended over a mile long with riders four abreast.[3]

In 1999, all arena contestants must be members of the Professional Rodeo Cowboys Association or the Women's Professional Rodeo Association. The old facility is gone and in its place is an 8.5 million dollar multiuse sport complex built with private donations.

The Man Who Listens to Horses:

> When the estate and city called on my father to manage the land [donated for the rodeo grounds], he agreed, and shortly thereafter construction began on more than 800 box stalls and a competition arena with a 20,000–seat grandstand. . . . My father, Marvin, also operated his own riding school on the grounds. . . . (p.37)

1937, SALINAS

Marvin Roberts stood in the street and blew his whistle long and hard as he raised an arm to stop traffic on Main Street.

The driver of the produce truck waved to Marvin who bobbed his head in acknowledgement as he continued to direct the steady stream of traffic across the busy intersection.

Marvin had taken the job directing traffic to help his friend, Bud Talcott, during a farmworker strike against the Grower-Shipper Association. Bud was striving to keep order in town. Tempers were short and the number of automobiles was increasing faster than the skill

---

[3] Burton Anderson, *The California Rodeo—A Central Coast Tradition.* (Salinas: Burton Anderson, 1997).

of the drivers. Traffic mishaps were an irritation that no one needed. Having Marvin help the drivers navigate the main intersections was working to ease traffic problems and emotional tension in town.

When his shift was over, Marvin entered the office to collect his pay and the course of his life took a turn down a new and positive path.

In 1937, the California Rodeo was a widely publicized event. Attendees and participants often traveled a great distance to take part. Among local residents, it was considered the event of the year. A riding club located at the rodeo grounds, however, was not faring so well. Nearly defunct, the club and a stable full of horses had been purchased by Salinas agri-businessman, Ellis Spiegl.

Spiegl happened to be in the office talking to Bud Talcott when Marvin reached the head of the line. "My daughter Ellyse is crazy for horses," Marvin heard Spiegl say to Talcott, "I want the club revitalized for the kids around here but most especially for Ellyse." Talcott was nodding that he understood.

Spiegl was unsure what to do with the school, the horses, and the entire perplexing situation, when Talcott looked up and saw Marvin. With just four words, Talcott made dreams come true. He pointed a finger at Marvin and said, "Ellis, he's your man."

Spiegl questioned Roberts briefly, then asked if Marvin would consider moving his family to a little house on the rodeo grounds and take over the school. The school would be Marvin's to manage as he saw fit if he was interested in the job.

That night when Marvin shared the news with Marguerite, her eyes welled with tears of joy. A home at the rodeo grounds and a life with horses: their prayers had been answered in a most positive and abundant way.

Marvin went to look things over at the first opportunity. What he found at the stable did not please him at all. His initial reaction to the poor condition of the horses and the facility was simply to close the gate and give the horses time to relax and gain strength. He told Spiegl the horses were thin and weak and in no condition to take on the strenuous task of teaching children to ride. Spiegl trusted Marvin's opinion and let him close the school in order to bring the horses back to a healthy standard.

Marvin and Marguerite reopened the school several weeks later in flamboyant fashion. The students arrived to find a large box standing next to every horse prepared for the class. Inside each box was a new saddle. They had the saddles wrapped in confetti, and Marvin said it looked like a snowstorm hit the corral before the kids were through. It was a great way to open the school.

Marvin and Marguerite lived at the rodeo grounds in a small two-bedroom house with their boys, Marvin Jr. and Larry. Marguerite's baby sister, Joyce, was a frequent visitor. The children were together so often and looked so much alike, that the relationship generally required an explanation. Many assumed they were siblings.

1937–1942, SALINAS

Whenever Frank Martins was at sea, one of Mame's chores was to drove a lumbering truck to the produce sheds to collect a load of culled vegetables for livestock fodder.

She put Joyce on the seat beside her every morning. Her first stop was at the stables, where she left her toddler with Marguerite. She picked Joyce up again after the day's final run. Often, she left her son Jim too, who was only five. Marguerite didn't mind. She loved having her sister and brother around.

As a toddler learning to speak, Joyce had trouble calling her nephew "Marvin." It usually came out sounding like "Marny" which evolved to "Monty." Others started using "Monty," and within the structure of the family, it helped create an easy distinction between father and son.

Once Joyce was old enough to attend school, she continued to spend nearly every weekend and most of the summer at the rodeo grounds with her sister, Marvin, and the boys. Joyce loved her parents, Frank and Mame, dearly, yet she loved Marvin and Marguerite just as much. For as long as she could remember, they were simply a second set of parents. Monty and Larry were like her brothers.

"Part of the joy of being raised with Monty and Larry," said Joyce, "was being around Marvin. He was always in a good mood. His glass was always half full, never half empty. He had a wonderful sense of humor and liked to tease and play little jokes on people in harmless ways. Marvin had a way about him that always made me feel safe. It felt as if no harm could ever come to me under his protection. I lived the young girl's dream of growing up around horses. Because of my sister and Marvin, I learned to ride, love, and care for horses. I never felt like an outsider or that they were doing me a favor. My sense was always one of belonging."

The Roberts' home stood surrounded by a facility created for Western-related sporting events like rodeo, horse racing, and horse shows. Several rows of box stalls for the horses were in front of the house. There were also a couple of corrals there, where lessons were given on a daily basis.

Visitors were always welcome, and the door to the house was rarely locked. In fact, if a student forgot to bring lunch, they could be found in the kitchen at noon, filling up with a generous portion of the meal Marguerite laid out each day. The smells of good home cooking, horses, and well-worn leather mixed to give the home a unique aroma that captivated the senses.

Behind the house was the racetrack, rodeo arena, and a huge concrete grandstand with wooden benches, filled each year during Big Week. Giant eucalyptus trees dotted the landscape and provided shade for the horses and humans below. Along with shade came the mess. There was never an end to the long peels of bark, leaves, and seed-bearing pods that the afternoon winds whipped from the giant trees and littered on the ground. With the wind and debris came the scent: the sweet aroma of eucalyptus mixed with the musky smells of horse, manure, hay, and grain, permeated the air over the rodeo grounds.

In the late spring and early summer, the skittish winds from the north and west brought a hint of freshly tilled soil or the awful, sweet, pungent odor from the Spreckels sugar factory. Dust lifted from the rich topsoil found its way through cracks, crevices, and open windows to coat the furniture. In winter, the mercurial wind came up the valley from the south bringing rain to the landscape—long parched through arid summers that left the hills a burnished gold longing for moisture—to again turn a lush verdant green.

When the wind rustled through the elongated leaves of the eucalyptus at the rodeo grounds, the trees danced a soft hula and sang with whispered sighs overhead. Nature set a stage there that absorbed the senses of anyone fortunate enough to succumb to its soothing power. It is little wonder that eucalyptus is used extensively in the healing art of aromatherapy. For Marvin and Marguerite Roberts, and all who visited them, the setting was heady.

The Man Who Listens to Horses:

> I can remember people saying, "That boy's just three years old"—but I could walk, trot, and canter a horse, do flying lead changes, and perform figure-of-eight maneuvers without a great deal of trouble. (p.37)

> My father soon noticed my riding abilities and made plans to exploit them. . . . I could be pushed to the limit. . . . [My wins] confirmed my father's belief: I was the child who would make the Roberts name famous in the world of show horses. (pp.37, 38)

From 1937 to 1942, the rodeo grounds was alive with horses and riders working together to improve their skills. It was the only way of life that Monty and Larry had ever known. They became accomplished riders at an early age. Living and working with horses was the life their parents practically gave them from birth. They were riding at two years of age and winning awards by the time they were four-year-olds. Marvin and Marguerite taught, out of respect for both the horses and their sons, that riding was not a hobby to be taken up or discarded on a whim, and they all worked diligently to strive to be the best.

Marvin and Marguerite's love of horses rivaled only their dedication to the virtues of faith, hope, and charity. Their dedication and determination was simply to help children and horses enjoy one another. With love, kindness, and a belief that mutual dependence exists between horses and humans, they were determined that life should be pleasurable for both. They focused on children and the horses those children would ride.

Interview with Larry Roberts, Monty's brother, 1999:

"Monty and I loved to ride. We were good at it and we liked to win. Our parents were busy with students and horses, but they always made time for us. When we were little, we were begging them to let us ride much more often than the other way around."

Interview with Jim Martins, Marguerite's brother, 1997:

"Some kids play baseball, or basketball, or hockey. We rode horses and played around the stable. Sometimes we took the horses on hunting trips and other times we went to a rodeo, or a horse show, or just out for a good ride. We worked cleaning stalls and doing other chores too. It wasn't all fun and games, but it was a good life.

"I'm a few years older than Monty. I agree that he rode horses from the time he was very young, but there is no way I will ever believe he was doing flying lead changes when he was three years old. I was there."

Interview with Ron Stolich, Roberts student, 1998:

"I remember Marvin used to say something like, 'Children and horses are alike; you have to have patience with both. If you want them to

retain what you taught, you must understand it can't be done in one day.'"

Interview with Ellyse Spiegl Burke, Roberts student, 1998:

"Marvin was wonderful to us. He used to take us for rides down to an area we called the willows. He had plenty of work to do, but he would take the time to play with us. We often played cops and robbers and had so much fun!

"Marvin would take along an old saddlebag, and whoever had the bag was the robber. The robber would hide and the rest of us would pretend we were the posse and try to find the robbers in the willows. Marvin always made it special for us. That is the kind of man he was."

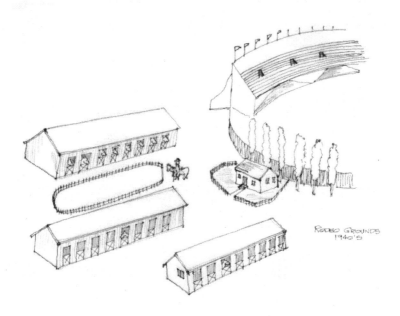

RODEO GROUNDS
1940's

Chapter 3

Hollywood

The Man Who Listens to Horses:

> It was 1939, and I was four years old . . . .
> (p.41) I cantered the gelding over the sandpit and
> took a dive off the right-hand side. The sporadic
> outbreak of applause was no doubt led by my father.
> . . . I had literally tumbled into the movie business,
> and over subsequent years I would appear in a
> hundred or so films. (p.43)

> I doubled for Roddy McDowall many times. . . .
> (p.43) I was Elizabeth Taylor in *National Velvet* . .
> . . I was Mickey Rooney, Charlton Heston, and Tab
> Hunter . . . . my father made all the decisions in
> dealing with the studios. He negotiated and signed
> the contracts. (p.44)

In the American book he said it started in 1939; he said 1940 in the British book. He would have been either four or five. Monty tells of being asked, and later directed, to fall off a horse. In time, he claims to have appeared in a hundred or so films, including *Thunderhead, National Velvet,* and *My Friend Flicka.*

Monty claims he doubled for the likes of Mickey Rooney, Charlton Heston, Roddy McDowall, and Tab Hunter. If his account were true, it would mean that Monty, then between the ages of four and perhaps six, was expected to double for much older actors.

Mickey Rooney was born September 23, 1920, fifteen years before Monty. Heston's birthday on October 4, 1923, makes him twelve years older. McDowall was born on September 17, 1928, six and one-half years ahead of Monty. Hunter, the closest to Monty's age, made his acting debut in 1952, when Monty was seventeen. It's hard to imagine that so young a boy could be used to portray the older actors.

Interview with Betty Dolan Kent, family friend, 1997:

"When I heard that Monty claimed to be a stand-in for Elizabeth Taylor, I was certainly surprised. Marguerite would have been in seventh heaven and would have been bragging to everyone about it. She would have been so proud."

Proud indeed, but *National Velvet* was only one movie. Monty said in an interview with Eric Brazil of the *San Francisco Examiner* that he worked on about thirty films, stunt riding for child stars in the early 1940s.

Brazil's article read: "I saw a camera, but I hardly knew it was a movie," he [Monty] said of his work on *National Velvet*. "I remember my dad saying, 'We're going to Mendocino County, and you're going to make the horse go over some jumps in a field.' We didn't know Elizabeth Taylor. Who had heard of her then? Nobody called the paper to say that Monty Roberts went to Mendocino County and jumped a horse over a fence."[4]

According to Mendocino historian Bruce Levene, no part of *National Velvet* was filmed near Mendocino.

[4] Eric Brazil, "Bio called unbridled fiction," *San Francisco Examiner*, (January 11, 1998, Section A, P.1, 18).

In *Liz, An Intimate Biography of Elizabeth Taylor*, C. David Heymann quotes Mickey Rooney, then twenty-three, Elizabeth's costar in the 1944 film:

> "Whenever they shot the jump scenes, Elizabeth sat on the sidelines. Billy Cartlidge, a stuntman with long hair who looked like Elizabeth, rode the steeplechase. It was he—and not she—who was thrown and whose back was injured."[5]

Interview with Jim Martins, Marguerite's brother, 1997:

"I can't imagine how Monty thinks he can convince people he was a stunt double. I know he never did that, because I was there. It's not like his life was a big secret. Besides that, Monty never liked to get hurt. He didn't like to ride steers, and he darn sure didn't want to ride a horse that might hurt him.

"The only stunt riders I know of in our family are my daughter, Marguerite [Martins Happy], her husband Clifford [Happy], and their two boys, Sean and Ryan. They've been in countless films and television shows.

"The walls of our house and theirs are lined with their photographs next to the stars they've doubled for. With all the pictures of my sister's boys, I would think that someone, somewhere, would have a picture of Monty in this capacity. One where it is clearly visible who the [stunt] rider is!

[5] *Liz, An Intimate Biography of Elizabeth Taylor*, C. David Heymann, (Carol Publishing Company, 1995).

"But we sure don't know of any [photos] and we never even heard about him being a stunt rider until his book came out. He never mentioned it when our kids got into that line of work, though we spoke often."

Interview with Angie Garcia, Marguerite's best friend, 1997:

"Marguerite confided in me about everything, and I in her. She was always so proud of her boys and everything they did. I know Monty never went to Hollywood and never did any stunts for the movies. Marguerite would have had it put in the paper; at the very least, she would have bragged about it to her friends. It's what she did."

Monty says his father exploited him for publicity. If that were true, why would Marvin keep this exciting news about Monty being a stunt double a secret from every single person that he knew?

Clifford Happy, Johnny Cash, Marguerite Happy, and Bill Hart on set of Dr. Quinn, 1996. (Photo courtesy of M. Happy)

A Cry of Abuse

The Man Who Listens to Horses:

My father's methods of dealing with horses were what I would describe as conventional—but that is to say, cruel. . . . The horses were . . . terrified. . . . They rolled their eyes and kicked, reared . . . . (p.39) Fear is in the horse's nature, and they were driven wild with it. (p.40)

Early in 1942 . . . . (p.46) I took the horses to a distant round pen . . . . [My father] took up position on the viewing stand . . . . (p.47) [After watching me, my father] raised the stall chain and brought it down hard, again and again . . . . I writhed in his grasp . . . . He whipped horses into submission and now he was giving me the same treatment . . . . I was put in the hospital . . . . The beatings continued weekly for three more years . . . . Only when I was fifteen did they cease . . . . (pp.48,49)

Marvin's horse training methods were not new in 1937 and they were not unique. Gifted horse handlers around the globe believe in gentle training. Just as licensed physicians no longer cling to the leech as an instrument of healing, most professional horse trainers discarded the philosophy of fear-based domination and cruelty years ago.

The current popularity of a trend called *natural horsemanship* is the progressive realization and continued evolution of those gentle horse training and communication methods. There are many wonderful and gifted horsemen and women who practice the art and training techniques associated with natural horsemanship.

Any and all information on these pages regarding various methods of horse training are not offered as the only way, or the best way, to start or train a horse. They are only offered to portray a clear picture of the training methods of Marvin E. Roberts.

Monty accuses his father of being physically abusive to him and to horses. Marvin is depicted as a cruel man who gained superiority through dominance over those he encountered, be that a horse in training, a wife, or a son with ideas of his own.

Those who knew the Roberts family were initially shocked by Monty's allegations. They were later astounded that such absurd lies could prosper while the truth was actually shunned.

Whatever the reason, there are millions of people who support and believe Monty Roberts. Perhaps because the human spirit longs for a survivor. The human spirit longs to believe.

Fairy tale stories take on a familiar pallor. The ogre is ugly, cruel, and seemingly angry. The victim gains strength through goodness to overcome evil. The victim rises to win in the end. Whether with the abused child or the misunderstood horse, Monty seems to employ this same theme.

His best-selling book delves into detail to describe Marvin as a man who abused and exploited his son's extreme talent. He describes Marvin as a person who trained horses through dominance, superiority, cruelty, and fear.

In a 1996 televised interview, Monty spoke of a father who was cruel and abusive to horses. With tearful eyes and a crack in his voice he told the audience he was beaten by his father when he was just seven years old because he wanted to train horses with gentleness and kindness. He said he was whipped with a chain and hospitalized due to injuries sustained at the hands of his dominating father.

Interview with Larry Roberts, Monty's brother, 1997:

"Monty was never an abused child. He and I shared a bedroom. Never once was there ever a hint of reason for me to think that he was being beaten by our father or by anyone else.

"Monty was very vocal about every little incident that he might consider an injustice against him. He would have screamed like a banshee if he were being beat. I know him. He can say whatever he wants to the rest of the world. But I know the truth.

"We used to take baths together. I never once saw a bruise that I didn't know exactly how Monty got it. As for my mother, if there were a definition in the dictionary for strong woman it would be Marguerite Roberts.

"I think our parents did more for the two of us then any parents that ever graced this earth. My dad was as thrilled as any father could be when Monty or I won or even placed in an event. For Monty to do what he has done to our deceased parents is darn near unbearable for me."

Joyce's Memoirs, Marguerite's sister, 1997:

"Monty talks about a round pen, but there wasn't a round pen anywhere on the rodeo grounds in those days and there wasn't any

raised platform or viewing stand from which Marvin would have watched him."

In a 1972 statement on file in the Superior Court of the State of California, Monty Roberts was asked if he had ever been hospitalized for any reason. He answered that he had been hospitalized in 1952 for an appendectomy.

Monty made no mention of any other hospitalization.[6]

Interview with Anita "Skeeter" Garcia Innocenti, Roberts student, 1997:

"In nineteen forty-six, I was five and started riding with the Roberts. I spent most of my days and many nights there through high school. Our families were so close that it's impossible for me to believe Marvin was abusive or domineering when he was alone with Monty or the horses.

"Our mothers were strong women. At the very least, Marguerite would have hinted or my mother suspected if there was trouble in that home. My parents would never have let us stay overnight if they thought Marvin was abusive to Monty or anyone else."

1941, Longing to Touch

A small boy used to stand near the fence and peer longingly at the horses. He watched the other children

---

[6] Monty Roberts, *"Hastings Harcourt, et al., -v- Marvin [Monty] Roberts,"* Superior Court of the State of California, for the County of Santa Barbara, (January, 1972).

ride and wished he could just pet one of the beautiful animals. He thought the horses were magnificent. So big, so shiny. He was eight. Old enough to know that Santa Claus was not going to bring him a horse, no matter how much he wanted one.

Tony Vargas was a child with limited opportunities in life. His family was poor. There would be no horse at Christmas. Still, he watched the horses every day and he dreamed of them every night.

It wasn't long before Marvin noticed the boy. "Some of these horses need to be exercised. Do you want to give us a hand?"

Tony rode whenever Marvin found a horse that "needed to be exercised," which was nearly every day. Tony paid attention when Marguerite explained proper horsemanship to the students. He listened to all that Marvin told him about training horses. He watched and he learned. Mostly, he was happy to be there. He was mesmerized by the manner in which Marvin and Marguerite interacted with the students. Later, Tony would say, "Everything they taught, they taught with a lot of love, and they always made it fun."

Several years later, when Marvin and Marguerite had more horses and students than they could handle, a man named Garth Lacey wanted to put another horse in training. It was a dilemma. Marvin hated to say no, but knew he didn't have the time to take on another horse. According to Tony, Marvin asked him if he wanted to help out and train the horse on his own.

Tony was thrilled to get the chance. He said that Marvin gave him free rein to train the horse as he saw fit and wished him good luck. Reflecting on that freedom, Tony today says, "That's just one reason that Monty's story about getting a beating because he wanted to train differently than his father doesn't hold up in my book."

Interview with Betty Dolan Kent, family friend, 1997:
"I watched Monty on the television show Dateline. *It was difficult to sit there and hear the lies he told. I was in and out of the Roberts home on a regular basis from nineteen forty-four to nineteen fifty-seven. From the number of hours I spent in that household, I would have been blind not to know if Marvin was beating one of his boys."*

MARVIN'S HORSE PHILOSOPHY

In his book, articles, and interviews, Monty Roberts' mantra continues with a steady whine that his father was cruel to horses and to him. He states repeatedly that Marvin's methods were abusive and that Marvin instilled fear in the horses he trained. Monty cites that a book written and published by his father in the 1950s depicts Marvin's use of ropes to gain supremacy over horses. Monty's message does not waver. He states with cocksure conviction that his father's methods were cruel. He says unequivocally that conventional or traditional training methods used by other trainers, even today, are cruel to horses.

Marvin did not instill fear in horses and he never beat his son. Marvin's horses loved and respected him as he loved and respected them. The horses that he trained performed with but the lightest touch of request from him. They did so willingly and were treated to the best of care.

Are there better ways to communicate with horses? Maybe there are.

Is it possible to gain the trust of a horse in thirty minutes? Perhaps it is.

Is it possible to trust a one-thousand pound horse with the life of a child after thirty minutes of communication with the animal? Monty's message seems to imply that it is. He is indefatigable in his promotion of his horse training system called Join-Up. He says that his goal is to make this a better world for horses.

Marvin's goal was undeniably to make this a better world for horses but also for humans and especially for children. He knew the bond between horse and rider to be unique and wondrous for both species. He knew that in order to gain the trust and confidence of a horse, or a child, he could not do it through fear or through intimidation. Marvin believed the only way to train a horse was to show the horse what you wanted and what was expected from him. When you showed him and he understood, the training began. It was not done in thirty minutes; nor was it done in thirty days.

Never, in all of Marvin's training, was a horse harmed in anger or meanness. Marvin did not *punish* a horse for a mistake, but a swift lesson was taught if a horse with bad habits endangered the life of a child.

Marvin did not trust a horse with a child if that horse had not first proven to be trustworthy.

It has been said there is a fine line between abuse and restraint.

The third edition of the *American Heritage Dictionary of the English Language* defines abuse:

a·buse *verb, transitive*
a·bused, **a·bus·ing**, **a·bus·es**
1. To use wrongly or improperly; misuse.
2. To hurt or injure by maltreatment; ill-use.
3. To assail with contemptuous, coarse, or insulting words; revile.
4. *Obsolete.* To deceive or trick.

noun
1. Improper use or handling; misuse: *drug abuse.*
2. Physical maltreatment: *spousal abuse.*
3. A corrupt practice or custom: *abuse of power.*
4. Insulting or coarse language: *verbal abuse.*

The same dictionary defines restraint:

re·straint *noun*
1. The act of restraining or the condition of being restrained.
2. Loss or abridgment of freedom.
3. An influence that inhibits or restrains; a limitation.
4. An instrument or a means of restraining.
5. Control or repression of feelings; constraint.

Words are powerful tools. Use of the words *abusive* and *cruel* elicit visions of angry and mean behavior designed to belittle, damage, injure, wound, harm, mistreat, batter, beat, dominate, or desiccate. All of which bring out the emotion of compassion for the object of the abuse and cruelty. We are a society cognizant of battered women, abused children, sexual harassment, and those who abuse power.

Most people do not think teachers, trainers, coaches, doctors, mentors, police, or guidance counselors are abusive or cruel. Yet they could be. They could hit, slap, kick, beat, punch, whip, or flog, and probably some do. But that would not be considered the conventional or tradi-

60

tional method used. As a rule, they would practice and promote restraint and discipline.

A kind and loving parent does not let a three-year-old child run into a street during rush hour traffic or touch a hot stove to learn that neither is a desirable action. Teachers do not tie their students to the desk and push the information into their brains—although sometimes they might wish that would work. The examples are endless. The idea is not to split hairs.

Monty Roberts has provided the world with an explanation of one way to communicate with horses.

For Monty to claim that his father was cruel to him or to horses is an abuse of language.

Joyce's Memoirs, Marguerite's sister, 1997:

"Marvin was the ultimate role model. In all those years that I knew him, I never heard him raise his voice or saw him raise a hand in anger to his wife, children, or horses. We heard stories of women and children who were battered and abused. We knew of horse trainers who used cruel methods and thought they could force an animal to work or perform. People like that were definitely around in those days, but Marvin was not one of them.

"Marvin was gentle, kind, caring, and probably most of all he was compassionate. He had a way of always making a person feel special. He did the same with horses."

Marvin's horse training methods are explained more thoroughly in Chapters 11, 14, and 16.

Chapter 4

1942, Salinas, A World War Brings Change

Marvin and Marguerite had found their niche when they fell into a harmonious life working with horses and children at the rodeo grounds. During the war, the government took over the rodeo grounds for military matters and the riding school had to be closed. Marvin took a job with the Salinas Police Department and the family rented a house nearby on the corner of Church and San Luis Streets. It was a cute little house with a huge magnolia tree in the yard. It had two bedrooms *(not three)* and a small alcove off the front room.

Monty and Joyce were seven years old. Larry was five.

By then, Marguerite's little brother Louis was twenty-one and had married a beautiful girl of German descent named Katherine. Marguerite's diminutive sister Tiny, at eighteen, had fallen for the dashing good looks of Requil Holt, a military pilot.

It was an era of romance and gallantry. Everyone was gung ho to fight a war and Marguerite's brothers were no exception. Three of the five enlisted. Bud and Hart joined the Army while Lou became a sailor. Her mother, Mame, was thankful that Allen at thirteen, and Jim, now eleven, were still too young.

Lou's wife, Katherine, and his sister, Tiny, were determined to do their part for the war effort. They both took jobs as telephone operators in Salinas. The phone company was not far from the house that Marvin and Marguerite rented, and Marguerite insisted the girls stay with them until they found a place of their own to share. They had already decided to be roommates until their husbands returned.

Tiny and Katherine moved in with Marvin and Marguerite and the little house on Church Street fairly hummed with action. The accommodations were adequate, but far from generous.

Marvin and Marguerite took one bedroom, Monty and Larry shared the second, and Tiny and Katherine bunked together on a roll-a-way in the alcove. The atmosphere was charged with energy and excitement. It was like a slumber party that lasted for several weeks.

Before long, a Victorian bungalow down the street became available. The rent was right. The house was perfect—darling in fact, and the girls would be close enough to visit daily and take advantage of Marguerite's generous culinary offerings.

Settling the Roberts family residence was one thing. But the Roberts had a stable full of horses too. Life without them was unthinkable.

The Man Who Listens to Horses:
> We moved to a small house . . . . [It had] three bedrooms . . . . horsemeat was required for the war effort. . . . bound for [slaughter] was my faithful red roan, Ginger. (pp.50, 51)

Scouring the area, Marvin found a small parcel of land with a large barn and corrals. It was on Villa Street near Market, not too far from the house on Church. There was enough room for the family horses plus a few extras. With a home for his family and a few of their horses, Marvin felt certain they could adapt to the circumstances and changes brought on by the war.

Not all of the horses could make the move to Villa Street. One of the horses that the boys used to ride and show was a red roan gelding named Ginger. Practically a member of the family, there was both sadness and joy when a new home was found for Ginger with a family down the valley.

"Ginger will have a good home," Larry remembers his father saying as they said good-bye and watched the family haul the horse away. "Daddy made sure that Ginger was spared death," said Larry.

Because of the war, Marvin was forced to send several horses to slaughter for the war effort. A horrible task for a man who loved and cared for horses as much as Marvin did, but Ginger and many others were actually spared this fate because Marvin found homes for them.

Accusations

Monty claims that when he was eight years old, he watched his father, then a policeman, severely and viciously beat a man, nearly to death. In fact, says Monty, the man was black, his father was a racist, and the man was given no medical attention and died two days later, presumably as a result of the beating by Marvin.

Readers get the impression the man was a soldier affiliated with nearby Fort Ord. The account is horryifying to anyone. It brought unbelievable pain and torment to those who knew it was a lie. It provided a strong incentive to write this book.

The Man Who Listens to Horses:
[It was] in 1943 [that] I saw my father [disarm a] black man in army fatigues . . . . [my father] caused the man to fall back, and his head cracked on the edge of the bar. . . . He lay motionless . . . . [my father] put the cuffs on . . . . [Then he] dropped, driving his knee into the chest of the unconscious

black man. . . . [Next, my father] slammed the heel of his cowboy boot into the mouth of the fallen man. . . . he grabbed the chain connecting the handcuffs . . . dragging the black man . . . . my father [was] surrounded by onlookers . . . . He gave the torso an extra lift and then released the chain, dropping the back of the man's head onto the sidewalk. (pp.54-58)

I could only see bubbles of blood around [the black man's] mouth. . . . At the station . . . . Other officers . . . laughed and hooted . . . . I saw my father kick him repeatedly in the ribs . . . . Years later, I was told that the black man had lain for two days with his ribs broken, his lungs pierced and his skull cracked. He died without ever seeing a doctor. (pp.59,60)

Larry Roberts tells his version of the abhorrent story.

Interview with Larry Roberts, Monty's brother, 1997:

"My brother claims that when our father was a member of the Salinas Police Department, he used his authority and power to cause the death of a black man during an arrest. In his book, Monty vividly describes the incident and says that he remembers the situation. [Monty also says that Larry was not there.]

"I'm familiar with the scene. I was there too. It happened at the Golden Dragon Saloon on Soledad Street.

"Regardless of what Monty says—we were both in the car with Daddy when he stopped [there] because of a disturbance.

"When we arrived, the crowd was holding a

man that had beaten up another man, who was lying on the sidewalk. I remember seeing my dad put a jacket or a blanket underneath the head of the downed man and handcuffs on the man the crowd was holding. The police came and took them both away; they had already been called before we got there and arrived minutes after we did."

There are no police records of any such arrest by Marvin Roberts and no witness has come forward to validate Monty's accusations. According to Monty, however, there were many witnesses: those at the saloon and several police officers.

In the February 1999 issue of *Horse and Rider* magazine, reporter Ronna Snyder wrote, "Dale Cheek, a former Salinas police officer who worked at the small-town police department with Roberts' father and ten other commissioned officers, is skeptical of this story. 'To accuse a police officer of killing someone with his hands and feet is a pretty serious thing,' he explains. Now the retired chief investigator for the state of Alaska, Cheek adds, 'It would have been hard to hide something like [what Roberts has written about]. And if I would have heard about something like that, I would have remembered it. This just couldn't have happened.'"[7]

The accusations leveled at Marvin are consistent with Monty's vile characterization of his father. A good fiction writer could not have developed a better bad guy to perpetuate the virtues of the protagonist. The accu-

[7] Ronna Snyder, "Horse Whispers–Or Horse Feathers:" *Horse and Rider,"* (February, 1999, P.58). At the time this book went into print, Monty Roberts had filed a $10 million claim against Ronna Snyder, *Horse and Rider*, and Primedia Publications.

sations against Marvin are wholly unfitting and unfair according to everyone who really knew him.

Sadly, people want to believe Monty was able to overcome an oppressed childhood and that he discovered a revolutionary way to communicate with horses and with humans. The truth is not nearly so glamorous.

Marvin Roberts in uniform, Salinas Police Department. (Photo courtesy of Larry Roberts).

Around 1943, Church Street, Salinas

The Man Who Listens to Horses:
"We're going to the fights," [my father in 1943] said.... [The boxer, Joe Louis] was the first of his race I had seen since the robbery.... My father was a racist.... (pp.61, 62)

Marguerite was adamant when she told Monty no. He was not going to go to the armory to meet the great boxer, Joe Louis. Larry was listening and praying he didn't get a fever before it was time to go.

"No. I'm sorry Monty, but you are sick and you're contagious." She smiled, "That means if you are around other people, they will get sick too. You don't want to make Mr. Louis sick."

"It's not fair. Does Larry get to go?" Larry heard his older brother ask his mother.

"Just to meet Joe Louis, Monty. He's not staying for the fight."

Monty claims that his father introduced him to Joe Louis and gives an account of their conversation. Larry, backed by Joyce, remembers that Monty had a contagious childhood disease and was upset that he couldn't meet Mr. Louis.

Monty never met the boxer. A photograph was taken of Larry sitting on Joe Louis' knee. A photograph that Larry says Monty took from the family album and never returned to his brother.

ELEMENTARY EDUCATION

Monty was always an exceptional student. Gifted with a desire to learn and an easy understanding of the subject matter, he did well. Larry, unlike his older brother, thought the entire thing was a waste of valuable time. When it came to school, any similarity between the boys ended.

Interview with Larry Roberts, Monty's brother, 1998:

"When Monty started going to school, I desperately wanted to go with him. He loved school so much and got very good grades. I remember Mom and Daddy were so proud of him. I tried to sneak out of the house with him once so

I could go to school too. Everybody laughed and told me I'd get my chance before long.

"Sure enough, the next September when it was time for me to go, I was up and ready. That very first day Mom and Daddy both took us to the school. I hated it. I really hated it. I did not understand at all why Monty thought it was so great.

"The next day, Mom drove us to school again. That day, she may have watched me walk in the front door, but she probably didn't see me walk right out the back. I wanted no part of school. I just wanted to go home.

"I walked. I don't know where Mom was. She wasn't home when I got there, and the house was locked. Our neighbors must have called Daddy at the police department to tell him I was sitting on the front porch.

"I remember Daddy came by and asked what I was doing there when I was supposed to be in school. I told him straight out I hated it and I did not want to go anymore. I guess Monty and I must have gotten our way a lot because I don't remember thinking this was anything I'd be in trouble about. Daddy just laughed and said, 'You have to go Larry. You can't quit school in the first grade.'

"He took me back to school that day, and I did continue my education. He was never angry with me about it, and I don't remember being afraid to share my true feelings with him.

"I was starting third grade when we changed

schools. Only a few blocks apart, the two schools were vastly different. For starters, the new school was a Catholic school, and we wore uniforms.

"The third grade at Sacred Heart was not too bad as I recall, but after the second day of the fourth grade, again, I did not want to go back. I had tried it, I had tried it some more, and I just knew that I didn't want to do it anymore. It was a plain and simple fact that I hated school.

"Daddy asked me what in the world I planned to do with my life. I told him I'd get a job at the police department. He thought about this for a bit and then said, 'Well okay.'

"So he took me to the police department and gave me a big stack of papers to fill out. He said I had to fill out all the paperwork before they could hire me. I took a pencil and got started. The problem being that I couldn't read half of it.

"Daddy left me with the papers but returned in a few minutes with a huge man in street clothes and told me to put the cuffs on this man and take him in. One look at that guy's leering face and I knew I was not going to be working at the police department for a few years. I had to go to school.

"When we got home, Daddy told me I'd better forget this notion I could quit school. He really meant it too because he told me I wouldn't get any extras until I got this crazy idea out of my head. I finally realized that I had to go to school and accepted it. I never did like it. Not like Monty did."

Dick Gillott lived about six blocks from the Roberts' barn on Villa Street. Approximately the same age as Monty and Joyce, Dick knew the family well because his much older brother, Wendell, had worked for them at the rodeo grounds before the war. When Marvin moved the horses to Villa Street, Dick and his friend Jimmy Barker started hanging around on a regular basis.

Interview with Dick Gillott, Monty's childhood friend, 1998:

"As a kid, I liked everything about cowboys and horses and wanted to be around them as much as I could. Jimmy Barker and I used to go to the barn on Villa Street to watch Marvin and the horses. We spent a lot of time at their home on Church Street too.

"We watched Marvin all the time and never saw him be cruel. Monty's description of Marvin is just not right. That's not how he was."

The Man Who Listens to Horses:

[Marguerite Parsons] was a central figure in my life. . . . She had been our baby-sitter since I was two or three years old, and now she became my teacher as well. . . . She would not leave us until 1949 when I was fourteen years old. (p.72)

1944, Betty Comes to Town

It was near the end of January in 1944 that Betty Dolan Mathiesen arrived from Los Angeles to visit her old school chum, Donna. By coincidence or fate, Donna lived on San Luis Street, right next door to Marvin and Marguerite Roberts.

Donna worked as a reporter for the Salinas newspaper and had the courthouse beat. One cold and wet winter day, Judge James A. Jeffrey asked Donna if she knew anyone who might like a temporary job.

Jeffrey needed an assistant, he said, but not for more than thirty days. Donna got excited and told him that her girlfriend was visiting from Los Angeles and said it would be wonderful to have her stay longer. With a telephone call to Betty, Donna changed the course of her friend's life.

Betty accepted the temporary job, staying with Donna and becoming good friends with their neighbors, the Roberts. Things were about to change, however.

Donna's husband, Al, was a soldier stationed at Fort Ord. When he was transferred to Salina, Kansas, Donna bid a tearful farewell to Betty and left Salinas with her husband.

After Donna left, Betty's job with Judge Jeffrey became permanent, and Marguerite and Marvin Roberts all but adopted her into the family.

Interview with Betty Dolan Kent, family friend, 1998:

"I was over at the Roberts house on Church Street for dinner at least two or three times a week. When dinner was over, I usually helped Monty and Larry with their homework.

"This was our routine from early in nineteen forty-four until late in nineteen forty-six. For nearly three years I spent a majority of my nonworking hours with the Roberts family. I continued a very close association with the family for the next ten years.

"I've been told that Monty refers to a woman by the name of Marguerite Parsons who was his

73

baby-sitter and tutor, but for the life of me, I can't remember anyone by that name. I simply can't imagine to whom he is referring. There certainly wasn't anyone by that name in or around the Roberts household after nineteen forty-four.

"I enjoyed watching Monty and Larry grow up. The boys were always with us and entered events at the various rodeos we attended on the weekends.

"Wherever the kids wanted to go to compete on their horses, Marvin and Marguerite took them. On several occasions, we even went over the Gabilan Mountains so they could compete against children in the San Joaquin Valley. I didn't work on the weekends, so they often invited me to go along.

"In nineteen forty-four, Marvin and Marguerite planned a big trail [horse] ride over the Santa Lucia Mountains to Carmel Valley. [Marguerite's sister] Tiny and I decided to drive over the mountain and join them for the evening. We arrived before the riders and watched them finish the long trip. They looked tired but sported huge grins showing white teeth that split their dusty faces. We celebrated with a big barbecue dinner.

"It was a good day. The kind of day to share with family and friends. It was a day that celebrated life, families, friendships, good times, and the horses. Always the horses were involved. Always the horses came first. Not one person ate *one bite of barbecue until those tired horses were fed, watered, and bedded down for the night.*

"I went to many, many rodeos and events with the Roberts and always had a wonderful time. Marvin used to drive a big brown car that had a huge back seat. Tiny, Katherine, and I sat in the back, and the boys sometimes sat on the floor back there with us. They would have two horses loaded in the trailer behind the car and off we would go. [Those were the days before seatbelts and before most people understood the possible danger.]

"On September first and second of nineteen forty-six, the Monterey County Sheriff's Posse

Betty became another one of Mame's girls. Here they are on Thanksgiving Day, 1946, at the Martins Ranch. Left to right: BettyDolan Mathiesen [Kent], Mame Martins, Tiny Martins [Holt], Marguerite Martins Roberts, and Joyce Martins [Renebome] in front. (Photo courtesy of Betty Kent).

75

held their first rodeo at the posse grounds on Natividad Road. The posse had purchased the land and began building the facility in nineteen forty-five. When the weather was good, members often stopped by after their regular jobs to help with the construction. On weekends, the grounds were a hive of activity. If Marvin wasn't working for the police department or taking his boys to a horse show or rodeo, he would be there too, hammering nails with the other members. Marguerite and I often made sandwiches for all the workers."

THE POSSE

The Monterey County Sheriff's Posse came to existence on February 28, 1939, when six Salinas men met and formed the Salinas Rodeo Riders and Sheriff's Posse of Monterey County. The six men were: C. D. Hansen, Sonnick Johnson, Jack Long, Jeff Parrish, Marvin Roberts, and Doc Watson. These six men had a vision.

The organization today has seventy members and supports a clubhouse and an arena for the continued promotion of horse-related events. In addition to riding as a group in several parades, the posse sponsors the annual Big Hat Barbecue in Salinas to kick off Big Week. They also sponsor a major junior rodeo that includes numerous horsemanship classes and is held at the posse grounds.

The Monterey County Sheriff's Posse does not chase criminals. They are a law-abiding group of citizens dedicated to preserving a western heritage for future generations.

The arena built by members in the early 1940s was refurbished in 1977. In a formal dedication service, the new arena was renamed in honor of one of its charter members who exemplified all that the posse stood for. A wooden plaque hangs over the entrance: MARVIN E. ROBERTS ARENA.

When he wasn't working with horses on Villa Street or doing construction at the posse grounds in the early 1940s, Marvin was a policeman. As his brother Ray describes him, Marvin was a man "always trying to help somebody with something."

Of the many people who had contact with him throughout his seventy-seven years of life, only his oldest son would one day describe Marvin as aggressive, cruel, or dominating. Most knew Marvin as a gentle human with a sharp wit, a generous attitude, and a loving heart. He made pets of all animals, even the livestock. For all living creatures, Marvin had omnipotent compassion. As a police officer, his philosophy of life, his demeanor, and his core beliefs were perfectly suited to protect and serve the community he loved.

SPRINT RACES

The Man Who Listens to Horses:

When I was eight, I started riding quarter horses in sprint races . . . . I had no serious accidents, despite riding in some 200 races . . . I did fall off a time or two, and I often rode without a protective helmet. (pp.62,63)

Interview with Larry Roberts, Monty's brother, 1998:

"Monty never rode in two hundred sprint

races! He might have raced a time or two, but he just wasn't into that. I raced a lot, but Monty never did. If Monty raced like he says, where are the pictures [of young Monty on a racehorse]? We have pictures of everything."

No one from Monty's past can remember that he rode in any races. By Monty's calculations, he rode in these races when he was between the ages of eight and thirteen. He infers that he did this at little towns up and down the state of California charging five dollars to ride and ten dollars to win.

These were the years that Betty Kent spent nearly every weekend with the Roberts; at home, at horse shows, and at the rodeos. Like the others, Betty remembers that Larry raced quite a bit. Neither she, nor anyone else, can remember seeing Monty ride a racehorse.

Interview with Betty Dolan Kent, family friend, 1999:

"I don't remember Monty riding in any sprint races when he and Larry went to the shows, but I do remember that Larry raced quite a bit."

Ronnie Koch helps Larry Roberts at the rodeo grounds. (Photo courtesy of Larry Roberts. Allmond and Parnell photo)

At the Martins Ranch

Monty asks readers to believe that as a child less than ten-years-of-age, he received weekly beatings from his father. He also states that Marvin would 'bloody his skull' if Monty erred or defied him. The majority of the beatings that Monty claims to have received came prior to, and during, World War II.

When the Roberts' lived on Church Street, our nation was at war and gas and sugar were rationed. The boys' lives revolved around school, friends, family, and always, always, their horses. Their grandparents, Frank and Mame, remained on their ranch with their three youngest children, Allen [aka Beek], Jim, and Joyce. Grandpa Martins continued to fish while Grandma worked at the ranch. Aunt Joyce didn't seem like an aunt. She spent so much time with Monty and Larry that she was much more like a sister.

Allen, Jim, and Joyce usually went to visit with the Roberts, but sometimes Monty and Larry came to play

The Martins home, circa 1943

at the Martins' ranch on Highway 101, just north of town.

After the confines of city living and the limited riding space of the Villa Street property, the exploration possibilities at the ranch seemed boundless. Everything at the ranch beckoned investigation by inquisitive young boys.

There was a shop behind the house and a small orchard off to one side. Way out back by the chicken pen, there was even an old comfort station that everyone called an outhouse. Left standing after the ranch house had been built with electricity and indoor plumbing, it was seldom used anymore but was convenient for boys playing outdoors.

A visit to the ranch also meant getting to spend more time with their Uncle Beek. Older and seemingly wiser, Monty and Larry were often awed by his knowledge of all sorts of interesting things. Beek had already started his own taxidermy business. He had a bedroom behind the garage and a second room next to the shop out back.

On one of their visits, Beek took the boys hunting with a BB gun. He had planned to teach them to handle a gun safely and to talk to them about the ethics involved in the sport of hunting.

Interview with Larry Roberts, Monty's brother, 1997:

"We'd been out shooting with Beek that day. When we finished, Monty headed toward the outhouse saying he had to use the facility and that he'd be right back. I went with Beek to his room and we put the BB gun away. Then Beek was showing me his taxidermy work and some things he had mounted when we heard this 'kah boom!'

"We knew better than to ever touch any guns without an adult with us, but there was Monty, holding a gun that was almost as big as he was. He had picked up the old gun in the shop on his way back and put the weapon to his shoulder. I guess he was pretending to be hunting and somehow he pulled the trigger because, all of a sudden, it went off.

"It blew a hole right through an old armoire where Beek kept his clothes! The three of us stood there in absolute silence for a few seconds, our eyes wide, staring at the hole in the armoire. When Beek and I turned toward Monty in shock and disbelief, he started to cry. That was the moment realization must have set in for all of us as to what could have happened. Monty begged Beek not to tell, but we couldn't keep that a secret.

In January 1999, Jim, Joyce, and Beek (in front), joined Hart, Louie, and Bud, in front of their childhood home.

When Mother and Daddy came to pick us up, we told them what happened.

"When we finished, Daddy took Monty aside and very calmly and very quietly explained how dangerous a gun could be. Grandpa Martins was there too. He was home from fishing at the time and we all got a lecture from him too. He told us something we would hear many more times through our lives. Grandpa Martins told us to always remember that a gun doesn't have a conscience; it kills whatever it's aimed at.

"Beek is the one who got in trouble over the whole thing because he was supposed to be looking after us. Neither Daddy nor Grandpa lost his temper or even got mad."

Interview with Beek Martins, Marguerite's brother, 1998:

"Something has happened to Monty and I don't know what! When he was young he spent time with us at our house. I taught him to shoot a gun. He couldn't wink his left eye, so I had him shoot left-handed. Those were happy times.

"In nineteen ninety-six, I called my nephew Larry to tell him Monty was going to be on the television show, Dateline. Rod Burden, Monty's father-in-law, had called to tell me about it.

"Monty's book was doing well in Europe and they were preparing it to be released in this country. Larry was very proud of Monty, as was the whole family. We were all excited to hear Monty was doing so well. I called everyone and told them to be sure and watch the program.

Though none of us had read his book [because it had not been released in the United States at that time], we understood it was about horse training.

"After watching the program, I was shocked and ashamed for my nephew. He had achieved such a wonderful accomplishment, but I could not understand why in God's presence Monty demonized Marvin the way he did. I called Rod back to see if he had an answer for me. Rod suggested that if I thought [the Dateline *interview] was bad, I should read the book."*

Part II

Riding with the Roberts

THE RED PONY

Having seen horses all his life, Jody had never looked at them very closely before. But now he noticed the moving ears which gave expression and even inflection of expression to the face. The pony talked with his ears. You could tell exactly how he felt about everything by the way his ears pointed. Sometimes they were stiff and upright and sometimes lax and sagging. They went back when he was angry or fearful, and forward when he was anxious and curious and pleased; and their exact position indicated which emotion he had.

—John Steinbeck

Chapter 5

1946, The Rodeo Grounds

They had good times on Church Street and at the Villa Street barn, but it was a happy day when the family learned in 1946 that they could return to the rodeo grounds and the life they loved.

It was decided Marvin would keep his position with the police department, and the family would help with the riding school. There was excitement in the air. A carnival atmosphere permeated Church Street as Marguerite carefully packed their few belongings and Marvin loaded the horses for the journey home.

The first order of business, once the family was back at the rodeo grounds, was to begin the cleaning process. They returned to find the grounds littered with nails and other dangerous objects. All needed to be removed for the safety of the horses and students. The entire Martins family and a huge contingent of friends showed up to help with the job. As testament to all that Marvin and Marguerite did for others, everyone came to help.

Coca-Cola Bottles

The Man Who Listens to Horses:
> [After the rodeo in 1947] it took [my brother Larry and me] two and a half months, working mostly at night, to [collect] 80,000 [Coca-Cola] bottles. . . . A convoy of trucks [took] the bottles away. Larry and I earned $800 each, then a small fortune. (p.78)

Like many children, Monty, Larry, and Joyce collected Coca-Cola bottles to earn the return deposit.

With so many people drinking Coca-Cola at the rodeo and around the stables, the bottles were scattered everywhere. Recycling was in its infancy when the Coca-Cola Company offered a deposit refund on returned bottles. One bottle put two-cents in the pocket of a resourceful individual who took the initiative to grab one that had been discarded.

It was a lucrative little business for the children after the rodeo. A few bottles here and there brought coins for candy or just a jingle to the pockets of their denim jeans. Jingling change was a sign of wealth and independence—even if it was just a few pennies. Money meant you could buy your own chocolate bar, licorice stick, bubble gum, or hard candy. Having money always impressed your friends. Maybe you would even share.

Finding the occasional tossed bottle certainly didn't make anyone wealthy. It was a lesson in resourcefulness for the youngsters: finding three Coca-Cola bottles got a nickel for candy with a penny to spare.

Interview with Larry Roberts, Monty's brother, 1998:

"After the rodeo, we found a lot of Coke bottles under the grandstands when we went looking for money that might have fallen there. A cleanup crew came to haul away the trash left after the show. When everyone cleared out after the last day, the place was a mess. Not just under the stands, but everywhere.

"The cowboys left trash around the bucking chutes, the roping chutes, and just about every place they gathered. The tops of the six-by-six

fence posts were ideal for a rider to put an empty bottle.

"My brother remembers that he proposed to Doc Leach of the rodeo association that he and I would voluntarily clean up under the stands in return for the stuff we might find there. He was twelve, and I had just turned eleven. That was our first summer back at the rodeo grounds, and it was wonderful. We were so happy to be back home. I remember the summer months of riding and showing the horses. I remember collecting Coca-Cola bottles for the change and making a few dollars for our efforts. It was fun. Life was good. We rode, we played; we took care of our horses and helped with chores.

"What we did not do, was spend the summer days or nights cleaning trash and collecting Coke bottles under the grandstands.

"We did indeed collect more than a few bottles, but nowhere near to the 80,000 Monty claims! Now that would have been memorable!"

1948, THE JUNIOR HORSEMEN

It was somewhere around 1948 that Marvin and Marguerite created an organization known as the Monterey County Junior Horsemen's Association (MCJHA). Most of those who rode at the stables became members. Some members didn't own a horse of their own, but rode the Roberts' school horses.

No one who wanted to join was ever denied membership. The club brought members together for monthly meetings and socials. It gave students the opportunity to learn how to responsibly run a meeting. Marguerite insisted everyone had to learn parliamentary procedure. The MCJHA provided a venue for barbecues, trail rides, and other events. They also rode as a group in the daily horse parade during Big Week.

Joyce's Memoirs, Marguerite's sister, 1997:

"I was about thirteen when Marvin and Marguerite formed the [Monterey County] Junior Horsemen's Association. They were not paid to do this. It took a great deal of effort on their part to plan rides, horse shows, barbecues, and other events for the members. Though it put a heavy demand on their time and pocketbook, they were never too busy for us.

"It was a special time. We grew up with memories of overnight horseback rides and ghost stories over an open campfire. All the while we were safe and chaperoned by two very caring people.

"Riding with the junior horsemen during Big Week was a yearly highlight for us. Marvin and Marguerite proudly led us down Main Street during the daily horse parade. We were just as proud of them.

"There would be forty or fifty of us, all of us with matching outfits, saddle blankets and all. The riders in the front row carried full-sized flags that were mounted in special little boots attached to our stirrups.

"It was an honor to get to carry a flag, and we usually rotated those positions each day. The

*number one consideration to be a flag bearer was
a gentle horse that knew Old Glory dancing over
his head in the afternoon wind was not a danger
from which to bolt or run."*

Marvin's horse training philosophy included a curriculum that helped a horse learn not to be afraid. Marvin did not want to see a horse jump and run in fear from a waving flag or an irresponsible motorist with a loud horn. The combination of a frightened horse and an inexperienced child was a disaster in the making. The horse is generally in a better position to survive the ordeal safely.

Marvin and Marguerite Roberts trained horses and riders, but they had a much greater impact on the hundreds of lives they encountered. It was their passion, their devotion to do more, be more, and give more, that brought students to their barn and opened young minds to the intrinsic values and virtues by which Marvin and Marguerite lived their daily lives.

Junior horsemen in the Roberts home. (Photo courtesy Larry Roberts. Allmond and Parnell photo)

91

Interview with Ron Stolich, Roberts student, 1998:

"Besides my parents, Marguerite and Marvin were the most important people in my life as a youngster. Marguerite would pick me up every day after school and on the weekends too. For a city kid this was a big deal. To be able to ride and hang out at the stables, to me, was like getting to go to camp every day.

"Most of the time I would pack a lunch to take along, but if I forgot, Marguerite would have a big cold-cut spread for us to make sandwiches. You never had to ask or wait to be invited. They made us feel welcome and very comfortable to just walk in the house and help ourselves.

"Monty and I were close in those days and there were many times that I stayed overnight with [the Roberts]. Monty and I were the same age. I still remember the bedspreads on the boys' bunk beds. They were tan and brown and had pictures on them of cowboys swinging ropes. Larry slept on the top bunk, and Monty slept on the bottom, and I slept on the floor.

"In all the days or nights [that I was in their home or at the stables], I never even heard Marvin raise his voice to Monty or any of the kids. There wasn't any meanness in the man.

"Marvin and Marguerite taught us much more than riding lessons. They taught us good sportsmanship, integrity, responsibility, and fair play. Through all the years that I knew them, one thing is certain, if I had a problem, they were there for me."

One of the local doctors in Salinas who stabled a horse or two at the rodeo grounds was Dr. McPharlin. Three of his children learned to ride there. Jim, Ann, and Mike rode a horse named Ribbon. Joyce Renebome laughed when recalling the McPharlin children and Ribbon, saying he was just the right size for everyone to practice trick-riding.

Interview with Ann McPharlin Komick, Roberts student, 1998:

"It seemed as though whenever I rode in the big blue horse van, it didn't break down. Marvin said I was the good luck charm, so I was awarded the honor of riding in the van when we went on an outing or to a horse show. It was rather an uncomfortable ride but a prestigious position.

"I can still see the pattern of the dishes they had in the house. Anytime I got in trouble I was sent to the house to clean and do the dishes. Two things would get you in trouble with Marvin and

Ann McPharlin [Komick] on 'Flirt.' circa 1952.

Marguerite: using bad language and being rough on a horse. You never treated a horse badly, or you heard about it. If the boys got into trouble, they had to clean up stalls. The girls were relegated to housework.

"I used to hurry home from school to get ready for Marguerite to pick me up for riding lessons at the rodeo grounds. I spent every day after school there and all day each Saturday. I still remember the yellow and brown jacket I wore on cold days.

"Marvin and Marguerite were very much like second parents to all of us. My own parents were very comfortable that I spent so much time there. They knew the caliber of people that Marvin and Marguerite were.

"My dad was a family doctor in Salinas since nineteen thirty-one. It was a small town then, and news traveled fast. Reputations were made over years and broken overnight. Never would my dad have allowed us to spend so much [time] with someone he did not have the utmost trust in.

"It was a thrill for me, many years later, to take my son Jim to Marvin for his first riding lessons. The memories I enjoyed were relived with him. The patience Marvin had with my son, who was a bit nervous climbing on the horse for the first time, reminded me of all the concern and patience Marvin and Marguerite had shown to me while I was growing up.

"A smile comes to my face when thinking of all the fun and good times we had at the rodeo

grounds, at horse shows, and at other gatherings. To this day, I have kept the card they gave me with a gift for my high school graduation. They were also there to share my wedding day in nineteen sixty-five."

Interview with Mike McPharlin, Roberts student, 1998:

"In the late forties, at a very impressionable young age, I had a yearning to learn how to ride a horse and to be a cowboy. Salinas being an agricultural community, it was easy to find a place to learn the art of horsemanship, and the place to learn was the rodeo grounds.

"Marvin taught riding and worked part time as a Salinas police officer. Marguerite drove around town in the woody station wagon, picking up all the kids and taking us back to the grounds to learn horsemanship and how to grow up and behave as the next generation of adults. I guess they did the job correctly, since all of us that I know of made it!

"Under the supervision of Marvin and Marguerite, I was taught to ride and get along with other people. Marvin and Marguerite believed that people are to be respected, and animals are to be treated the same. Over the years, until the mid-fifties, I spent many hours there, participating as a member of the [Monterey County] Junior Horsemen's Association and attending horse shows in the area. From the Sheriff's Posse Grounds, to the Pattee Ranch Arena in Corral de Tierra, to the greatest rodeo

of all, the California Rodeo, I went with the group and with Marvin and Marguerite. At these shows, I was always under the supervision of the Roberts.

"One of the greatest treats that we kids were given, if everyone behaved, was a ride to the willows, located behind the county hospital off Natividad Road. This was where the training paid off. It was an area where we could play games such as tag or hide and seek on our horses.

"Another exciting adventure with the Roberts family was the trail ride up Fremont's Peak, an overnight camp out. There was never a dull moment with the Roberts, as long as one behaved and remembered the standards set by Marvin and Marguerite.

"My wife and I believed in the ability of Marvin to teach horsemanship. We took our son to him years later. To this day, we look back with fond memories of the hours we spent with Marvin and Marguerite and our friends from the stables. It's really a shame that this type of environment is not available today for the youth of Salinas.

"Possibly gangs would not exist, and if they did, it would not be ones of violence, but ones of competition. Shooting would be out and ribbons in. Maybe, just maybe, Salinas could return to the town that it was in the fifties."

When the school reopened after the war, students ranged in age from three to adult. Many possessed a competitive spirit and wanted to compete in the show ring, others simply enjoyed a good ride. It was the job of the coach to offer guidance and training. Competition meant work. The Roberts were quick to let an athlete know that in order to win, it would take hours and hours of preparation.

The thrill of victory is a powerful incentive. Just as a coach might watch his team win a championship, Marvin and Marguerite were always ringside, watching their students compete and win. Among the winners were their two sons who literally rode horses before they could walk.

MORE ABOUT EDUCATION

The Man Who Listens to Horses:

Schooling for Larry and me was cut back to bare bones. . . . (p.69) I was only in school for between ten and forty percent of the normal time [after we returned to the rodeo grounds] . . . . (p.70)

School is an important part in the life of child. From the basics of reading, writing, and arithmetic, comes knowledge. We learn at different levels. Some find it an easy task, while others struggle with seemingly simple concepts. In school, from the sandbox to the chemistry lab, we gain knowledge, develop our social skills and behavior, and prepare for life in the working world of adults. School is the training arena for life. Not all of the lessons learned are pleasant.

In addition to school lessons, Larry and Monty Roberts were learning life lessons at home. Anyone who has ever owned a pet knows that with pet ownership comes responsibility. With horse ownership comes even greater responsibility.

The Roberts were in the business of caring for horses: horses that belonged to their students; horses brought in to be trained by Marvin; horses used for schooling young riders; and horses owned, shown, and loved by the Roberts family.

When all the cowboy veneer and romance is stripped away to reach the truth of the matter for all to understand, this last group of horses—those owned, shown, and loved by Marvin, Marguerite, Monty, and Larry Roberts—were their pets.

Monty and Larry shared in the work of caring for their horses. Their life was not like the lives of children without horses or even those who boarded their horses at the stables. Their chores were important. Their horses depended on them. Marvin and Marguerite taught responsibility to their students. They instilled it in their sons; it was expected. The boys had horses, and they had the responsibility of caring for their horses. While they had responsibilities at home, the boys had responsibilities at school like other children.

Enrolled at Sacred Heart School after the war, Monty's attendance records between 1945 and 1949 are still on file. Monty claims he attended school only between ten and forty percent of the normal time, yet records show he was actually there more than ninety-five percent of the time.

A little whisper, a little lie designed to nurture the image of an eleven-year-old boy as a slave to his father. A little lie to perpetrate the picture of Marvin as the grueling taskmaster of the overly burdened lad who, despite the rigors of his life, maintained near straight-A grades.

Two of Marvin and Marguerite's closest and lifelong friends were Henry and Angie Garcia. The Garcia's settled in Salinas in 1935 and established the Garcia Saddlery Company. The changes brought by the war touched everyone, and the Garcias were no exception. In 1941, they closed the shop in Salinas to reopen in busy San Francisco. As war raged and the population grew, the Garcias longed to return to their friends and the gentle life they had known.

In 1946, this jubilant couple in The City by the Bay loaded their two young daughters, household possessions, and an entire store of leather goods for the move back to Salinas. Immediately calling their old friends, the Roberts, they met for dinner and talked into the night. After nearly five years, there was a great deal of catching up to do. From then on, the couples were inseparable until death.

The Garcia name became synonymous with quality leather and silver goods in the Western horse industry on the west coast. The names of Henry and his brother Les are well known to many.

Interview with Angie Garcia, Marguerite's best friend, 1998:

"Marvin and Marguerite Roberts were truly our very best friends. We owned Garcia Saddlery, and either Marvin or Marguerite would be in the store just about every day. Monty and Larry used to watch the craftsmen making saddles and bits. They'd sit for hours and watch Jay Valenzuela do his beautiful hand-tooled leatherwork.

"We used to go to Inter-Club dinner meetings together once a month all over Monterey County.[8]

---

[8] Inter-Club was a combined organization of several area clubs for horse enthusiasts.

We'd travel from King City in the south to Carmel or Monterey with the Roberts.

"At least twice a week, we got together with Marvin and Marguerite for dinner. One day at our house, the next at the their [house]. All the children loved Marvin—not just mine. He got along with everyone because he was such a genuinely good person. There is just no other way to describe that man.

"Our two families often went out to the Laguna Seca area to ride and work cattle with Vivian and Ralph Carter there. We'd also go to Moss Landing Beach where we'd dig for clams. We all worked hard, but we had fun too."

The Garcia's oldest daughter was five when the family returned to Salinas. Christened Anita, everyone called her "Skeeter." Pulling on her cowboy boots every day to ride at the rodeo grounds became a way of life for the dark-eyed little beauty. Her Spanish and Indian heritage was evident in her high cheekbones and translucent complexion. She rode well and practiced the lessons Marguerite shared with her every day. It was not long before the five-year-old was competing at shows with the rest of the students who rode with Marvin and Marguerite. One of the youngest to show, Skeeter was undaunted in her efforts to do well.

Interview with Skeeter Garcia Innocenti, Roberts student, 1998:

"The first horse that Marvin put me on was a wonder horse named Black Beauty. I believe that

many, many children started out riding Black Beauty.

"Most of the kids that rode there belonged to the [Monterey County] Junior Horsemen's Association. I remember those treasured memories of the overnight trail rides to Fremont's Peak, Holman's Guest Ranch in Carmel Valley, and Moss Landing Beach. It was exciting to ride in the surf while the grownups were digging for clams.

"The Grand National in San Francisco was one of our favorite horse shows. On Sundays there, Marguerite would take all of us kids to church before our classes at the Cow Palace. We would be dressed in our boots, hats, and leather chaps. I remember walking down the aisle at church trying to tiptoe so my spurs wouldn't jingle. Meanwhile Marvin and my dad got the horses ready for us to ride immediately after church.

"After the horse show, we'd all go to the Oliver Restaurant for dinner. Whether we won or not, we still celebrated. Marvin and Marguerite were always proud of all their students.

"I also remember Sunday nights after the local shows. After feeding the horses, we'd go to Joe Gregg's Airport Barbecue Restaurant for dinner. Sometimes there would be ten to fifteen people for dinner. Marvin and my dad bought Shirley Temple drinks for all of us kids, always with two cherries, and gave us money to play the jukebox.

"Marvin trained all my horses. I showed them

from February at Fairfax to the Cow Palace in November and rode every day, rain or shine. After school, Marguerite picked me up at the saddle shop, and my parents picked me up at the stables when they finished work.

"On Saturday mornings, our family went to the rodeo grounds where Marguerite fixed breakfast for us. Mom and Dad would have a cup of coffee then go on to work. I stayed all day. I rode, bathed my horses, and got equipment ready for the next horse show.

"It's hard to measure all they did for us, because they did so much. At noon, if Marguerite didn't have a feast prepared, she'd go to Roy's Drive-In and buy hamburgers for everybody.

"Marvin drove a big blue van and hauled all of the student's horses to the shows every weekend. He and Marguerite didn't just enjoy doing things for us, they loved it. We were their life."

1948, CHURCH STREET, SALINAS

On one occasion, Marvin's intuition and quick response may have saved the lives, and most certainly the emotional lives, of his sisters-in-law, Tiny and Joyce.

The night it happened, Marvin was working as watch commander at the precinct. Tiny was at home with her infant daughter, LaVonne, while Requil, home from the war, was working nights. The couple had taken over the house on Church Street, and the Roberts were again living at the rodeo grounds.

102

Being a Saturday night with no school the next day, Tiny had asked Joyce to stay and visit. Her husband had been working nights, and she felt uncomfortable lately, swearing she'd been hearing things. She didn't want to be alone and asked Joyce if she would stay the night.

Delighted for the opportunity to help her sister with the new baby, twelve-year-old Joyce agreed.

For nearly a week, Tiny had thought she heard someone or something outside the house at night. Each time, she called the police department, thinking she had a prowler. Each time, Marvin had answered the call and dispatched an officer to check it out. No one was seen, and they were starting to tease Tiny about her paranoia. Joyce was only twelve, but at least Tiny didn't feel alone and vulnerable.

Joyce was asleep in the second bedroom and little LaVonne was in her bassinet in the alcove. It was a quiet night, and they had gone to bed early.

Wakened by a sound at the window, Tiny opened her eyes to see a man there and the window starting to open. Her scream did not stop the intruder. In an instant, Tiny was out of bed as she thought of her daughter and Joyce.

Joyce woke from a deep slumber to hear Tiny shouting for her to get up. Jumping clumsily out of bed, Joyce fumbled in the dark toward the other bedroom.

She nearly collided with Tiny in the semidarkness. Neither of them had turned on a light. The only illumination was an eerie cast of moonlight through a window in the living room.

Tiny told Joyce to take LaVonne and go into the bathroom; then she reached for the heavy black telephone.

Joyce scooped up the baby and ran to the bathroom where she held LaVonne tightly against her chest and cowered in the corner. *Please Heavenly Father, let Tiny be safe. Don't let anything happen to her.* Joyce was only twelve years old. Her Catholic catechism lesson sprang to mind as she prayed for help.

She had never been so afraid. It was like the bogey man was coming. Only he was real. *What would he do?*

Joyce felt like she was choking. Her mouth was dry. Her legs felt thick and heavy. *What now? Oh, Dear Lord, what now?*

Tiny dialed the memorized number of the police department and screamed into the mouthpiece that there was a man in her house.

In the dim light, she saw the bedroom door start to open. Without waiting to see the intruder, Tiny dropped the receiver and bolted for the bathroom.

Inside, she latched the door and joined Joyce and LaVonne. Together they huddled and prayed that Marvin had been the one to answer and that he had recognized Tiny's voice. They prayed an officer would get there soon. They prayed that God would keep them safe.

They heard the siren. God had heard their prayers.

Marvin later told the rest of the story:

"She didn't say who it was or where they were, but I was pretty darn sure it was Tiny on the line," he said. "She had been pesterin' us all week about a prowler. For a minute, I thought it was a joke, the way she hung up so quick and all. But Tiny wasn't one for practical jokes. Besides, we never told her about it before, but we had had several robberies and rapes around that time. She and Requil were living in our old house, right around the corner from the station. Just to make sure they were all right, I sent a car over to check on 'em."

The siren may have been the deterrent. A man was on his way out of the window when the officers pulled up. In his hand, he clutched the gun from the dresser drawer that neither Tiny nor Joyce had been able to reach.

Joyce remembers that Tiny was asked to identify the man and testify against him. The robberies and rapes ceased. Requil was especially thankful that Marvin had had the watch command that night.

Marvin and Marguerite (left and right) at the wedding of Requil and Tiny Holt. circa 1946. (Photo courtesy of Lavonne Holt Kelly. Gainsborough photo).

Chapter 6

GRANDPARENTS

The Man Who Listens to Horses:

My father told disparaging stories about [his mother] and was not pleased that I sought her company. She was forbidden fruit. My grandmother spoke little English . . . she never said anything in front of my mother, but she seemed to come alive when we were alone together and she would rattle on in Cherokee . . . . (p.67)

Interview with Larry Roberts, Monty's brother, 1998:

"We used to drive over the mountain to Tulare to visit with our Grandpa Roberts who had moved there after our father was grown. Tulare was a small town when we were young. I think Grandpa was a sheriff, dog catcher, and jailer all in one. I remember him as a gentle and caring man, and our visits there were always something Monty and I looked forward to.

"He had also remarried after Daddy was grown. His wife, our step-grandmother, was a nurse. She was very orderly and seemed far more sophisticated than Grandpa.

"Once I asked Daddy right out, 'Where is your real mother?' I was curious and no one had ever talked about her. He avoided the answer, but I kept pushing until Mama finally took me aside

one day and told me there was a problem years and years ago. It seems that my dad's mother left the family many years before, and Daddy didn't know where she was.

"The war was over, and we had moved back to the rodeo grounds when Mom called Monty and me to the house to tell us our grandmother was coming to visit. I thought she meant Grandma Martins, who came over a lot and always brought Joyce. But she carefully explained to us that it was Daddy's mother, Daddy's real mother, who was coming.

"When Monty and I started to ask all kinds of questions about her, Daddy left the house and walked to the barns. Mama tried to explain to us that Daddy hadn't seen his mother for many, many years.

"We watched through the window as he took the first horse out of the stall, groomed him, put him away, and went to the next stall. He groomed each horse down the line, talking to them, giving each a bit of grain. That's what he always did when he was troubled about something: he went to the horses.

"The horses loved Daddy. Whenever he approached the stables, noses appeared over the tops of the stall doors. They would call to him with lots of nickering and vie for the affection and attention he gave to each of them.

"She arrived later that same day with my dad's sister, Alice, and his older brother, Lester.

It seemed they were only there for a few minutes before they started to talk about leaving.

"I remember asking, 'Aren't you going to stay and eat?' Everyone who came to visit stayed to eat. My mother always put on a big spread and insisted on feeding everybody.

"The atmosphere was different that day. Mama answered, 'Your grandmother has to leave now, Larry. They have a long way to go.'

"The one thing I remember about my dad's mother was that she had a little can of chewing tobacco. I had never seen anything like that before, and I wondered what that was all about.

"As I recall, they didn't stay for more than about fifteen minutes. Monty and I said hello to her, and that was about the extent of it. I don't think she even gave us a hug. Hugs and kisses by [female relatives] were not something you could wrangle your way out of around the Martins family.

"That was the only time I ever met our Grandma Roberts. I sure don't know when Monty spent time with her like he says in his book. He never did when we were living at home, and it's not something he ever told me about later."

Boxcars, Tutors, & Grooms

The Man Who Listens to Horses:

My father . . . leased a railroad car [at the end of the war] . . . . For the next few years, this railroad car would crisscross the United States. It was my home away from home during long spells in summer. (p.71)

Traveling in the car [to horse shows] with me were my favorite horse, Brownie; anywhere up to eight other horses; a groom (sometimes Wendell); and Miss Marguerite Parsons. (p.72)

As Monty would like you to see it, it's a romantic vision: the small boy and his well-trained show horses gently rocking to the rhythm of the train as it meanders through the country. Exploited and abused, he holds training clinics when the railcar stops for a horse show.

His talent with horses is legendary, though he is still just a boy. The clinics help finance the expedition and pay entry fees at the next horse show on the line.

His female chaperone helps him with his studies and keeps the financial records for the travelers. Her presence is essential because the boy is able only to attend school about ten percent of the time.

At home, he is badly mistreated and forced to clean twenty-two box stalls each day before breakfast. Yet traveling in the railcar, he is provided with a full-time groom, an advance scout, and a full-time chaperone and tutor.

In this history created by Monty Roberts, the boy is overworked, exploited, and abused.

In reality, there was no railroad car converted for his use. There was no railcar built to haul this young man and his horses from show to show. He claims the rattling wooden structure was his home during the summers, yet no one who was around Monty or his family during that time has any recollection of any of this.

What they do remember is that Monty did enter and win at many of the horse shows. He was always an excellent showman.

110

His horses were hauled to the shows, along with those of the other children that rode under the tutelage of his parents, in a blue moving van.

The truth is a vision that warms the heart—the hero is not the boy in the boxcar, but the man and woman in the old blue van.

All week they trained horses while their students were in school. After school, they coached and encouraged good horsemanship and taught valuable life skills. On weekends and through the summer months, they hauled horses and children in an old blue van to nearby shows.

Saddles and tack, brushes and combs, hats, boots, bridles, and britches were neatly organized and ready for student use. As trophies and ribbons were won, whoops of joy and laughter echoed through the tight-knit group of horses and riders from the rodeo grounds stables. When they weren't so lucky, when someone else had a better day, Marvin and Marguerite always had an encouraging word to share.

"We can't all be winners all the time," one, or the other would say.

There were no clinics put on by the boy or his parents. Certainly none that anyone *paid* to attend.

What could be found was a dedicated family—dedicated to helping horses and humans enjoy one another. They offered words of encouragement or suggestions for others to improve. They weren't looking to increase business. Theirs was a love that transcended the issues of money and notoriety—a love of humanity and of horses. Marvin and Marguerite brought out the best in both.

The van didn't always make it to the show. Sometimes it broke down. It had seen better days, but served its purpose—most of the time. But between the van and a station wagon they had, students and horses usually managed to get to the shows on time.

When the Roberts and their students were at a horse show, it was common for them to give last minute warm-up lessons at the show grounds. By the time he reached his midteens, Monty would sometimes help his parents and offer suggestions for improvement to other riders.

Larry Roberts and Joyce Martins Renebome remember Marguerite Parsons as a young woman or girl who baby-sat them only occasionally, when they were very small. Betty Kent doesn't remember the woman at all after 1944, and Betty was with the family almost daily until 1949. Monty says that he remember Miss Parsons as the tutor and chaperone who traveled across the country with him in a nonexistent railcar.

Wendell Gillott worked for Marvin both before and after the war. Wendell's younger brother, Dick, laughed when he heard the story of the railcar. Dick, like everyone else, knew the story was a fabrication.

In addition to Miss Parsons and Gillott, Monty claims his father employed an "advance man" who scouted venues and sold tickets to a clinic where Monty would "show you how to win" after the horse show. Like a young evangelist, he says, he traveled the country preaching. Only, he didn't.

Another whisper—another lie.

Strangely enough, it is similar to what he does now.

1948, RODEO GROUNDS

The year 1948 would have to be considered a benchmark in the life and times of the Roberts family. It was a year packed with activity and marked by new begin-

nings—and unforgettable lessons. It was a year to remember.

Interview with Bill Whitney, Marvin's horse shoer for forty years, 1997:

"I was at Marvin's place every Friday for
pretty near forty years. I watched his boys grow
up and all those kids that used to ride there.
Marvin was a special man. He had a way about
him that was gentle and kind. I would call him
a gentle man.

"Two incidents, in particular, come to mind
when I think of Marvin Roberts. They both
represent a bit of the measure of the man. The
first was at the rodeo grounds.

"I was putting shoes on a horse that just would
not stand still. I suppose I was getting more and
more frustrated, because about the time the horse
jumped away for the umpteenth time, I hit him
in the belly with the rasp and called him a
knothead or some such name and told the blamed
horse to stand still.

"Marvin almost fired me that day. He told me
that I was never, under any circumstances, to
hit any horse [again] at the rodeo grounds or that
day would be my last.

"The second memory that comes to mind after
all these years is a fishing trip he and I took up
to the mountains. We were way back in the hills
and it started to rain. Marvin got so concerned
about some horses that were in a corral without
a cover that he made me drive him some thirty

miles or more to a pay phone, so he could call and check on the horses. He was reassured that everything was fine, but he never relaxed and had a good time. He just kept going on and on about those poor horses and how he should have had shelter for them."

Interview with Jim Martins, Marguerite's brother, 1998:
"I do remember one time when Marvin got mad at me. I had never seen him mad or even angry before.

"On this occasion, he actually gave me a spanking. He didn't do it out of meanness, and I had no thought of abuse. It was an old-fashioned spanking, and I guess I had it coming. Anyway, I sure remember it well. Here's what happened.

"I was wearing a brand new pair of cowboy boots. I was real proud of those boots. I was helping Wendell clean the stall of this palomino horse when the horse reared up and came down on the toe of my new boots. I lost my temper and kicked the horse right in the belly.

"Well, Marvin saw the whole thing. He tore into me and gave me a spanking and said that it didn't matter what that horse did to my new boots or to me, I was never, never to treat a horse like that again. I never have."

WILD MUSTANGS

The Man Who Listens to Horses, 1997:
"What if," I proposed [in 1948] to Doc Leach

114

[president of the California Rodeo Association], "I go to Nevada and get the mustangs [for the wild horse races held at the rodeo]?" (p.5)

[I told Doc that] "I know I can ask for help from the Campbell Ranch." Bill Dorrance, a remarkable horseman in his mid-fifties who would become my mentor, had contacts at the ranch and would make the arrangements. . . . [I suggested] that after the rodeo Larry and I could break in the mustangs . . . . (p.5)

Doc Leach shifted his pipe from one corner of his mouth to the other . . . . Finally, we agreed that the net proceeds of any sales [from the wild horses] were to be divided equally between the rodeo association and the Roberts brothers. (pp.5,6)

Interview with Larry Roberts, Monty's brother, 1997:

"Why it's just plain nonsense to think Doc Leach agreed to let my brother be responsible for getting those horses when [Monty] was only thirteen years old, or that Doc had Monty and me break them later and sell them at an auction."

When asked about the matter, a current member of the California Rodeo Association, Pete Silacci, said that Doc Leach didn't have anything to do with the wild horses at that time.

Doc Leach was not president of the association until 1953 and though it's an insignificant matter, Doc's son, retired judge Jim Leach, told a reporter that his father never smoked a pipe.[9]

[9] Ronna Snyder, "Horse Whispers–Or Horse Feathers:" *Horse and Rider,"* (February, 1999, P.59)

Interview with Steve Dorrance, Son of Bill Dorrance, 1998:

"After hearing about Monty's book from others, I expected a signed copy for my dad [Bill Dorrance]. After all, he was mentioned as being one of Monty's teachers. Not receiving one, I purchased the book for Dad to read.

"After reading the first sixty pages, he told me there was not enough truth in the book to continue. There did not seem to be any point to him to read further.

"It's not a big deal, but he's got my dad's age wrong too. If Dad were in his mid-fifties in nineteen forty-eight, then he would be well over one hundred now. My dad is in his nineties, and he just finished writing his own book about horses."

The Man Who Listens to Horses, 1997:

> In June 1948, Ralph and Vivian Carter and I put our horses and our equipment in the van and headed off [to gather the mustangs]. . . . (p.6)

Published earlier in the United Kingdom, Monty wrote:

The Man Who Listens to Horses (U.K. printing, 1996):

> So come June 1948, Dick Gillott, Tony Vargas, my brother and I put our horses and our equipment in the . . . .(p.68)

Later, in the paperback edition released by Ballantine Books in 1999, the sentence became:

The Man Who Listens to Horses (First Ballantine Books Edition, January 1999):
> In the summer of 1948, the Carters and I put our horses and our equipment in the . . . . (p.4)

Interview with Dick Gillott, Monty's childhood friend, 1998:
> *"What? That's impossible. How could he say that? I never went to Nevada to gather any wild horses with Monty. Neither did Tony or Larry. Monty didn't go anywhere to gather or observe any mustangs during those years. I spent nearly my entire childhood around him. I would have known if he had done something like that."*

Interview with Tony Vargas, Monty's childhood friend, 1998:
> *"I'm trying to figure out who was supposed to be driving. I'm the oldest, but still didn't have a [driver's] license in June of nineteen forty-eight. The whole thing is a joke. Dick, Larry, and I all know we never went to Nevada with Monty to gather any wild horses. So before they print the book here [in the United States], he changes [the characters] to Ralph and Vivian [Carter] who, like his own mother and father, are dead and can't say they weren't there either."*

Interview with Larry Roberts, Monty's brother, 1998:
> *"My brother never went to Nevada to gather*

any wild mustangs with me or the Carter's or anyone else. The only place [that I know of] that Monty spent time watching wild horses [when we were young], was at the rodeo grounds when they were penned in the green corrals, right before Big Week."

Pete Renebome, Ronnie Koch, Dick Gillott, Larry Roberts, Tony Vargas, and Jim Martins in 1998. (Photo courtesy of Tony Vargas).

The Man Who Listens to Horses:

[After the rodeo] Larry and I had just sixty days . . . to break [the horses] . . . . (p.14)

My aim was to refine a technique that used the horse's respect and cooperation, not the one that forced its servitude. . . . I had chanced upon something new that would change the way human beings relate to horses. . . . I had come to think of my process as entirely different from that of "breaking" horses. . . . I changed the nomenclature. From that day on, I called my method "starting" horses. (p.14)

No one in 1999, including Monty, has explained why a full-color, glossy, tri-fold brochure for Monty's Flag Is Up Farms, contains the following statement:

"Talking with Horses. See Monty Roberts' method of breaking horses . . ."

Interview with Larry Roberts, Monty's brother, 1997:

"Neither Monty nor I had anything to do with any training or selling of any wild horses after the rodeo."

The Man Who Listens to Horses:

[In 1948, on this same trip to Nevada] Brownie was my number-one saddle horse, but in addition I had [a horse named] . . . Oriel. (p.8)

[In 1949] for three weeks I would be alone in the Nevada desert with the mustangs. . . . Once again, I was glad to have Brownie [to ride] for this all-important experience. . . . Oriel . . . walked along behind . . . . (p.16)

Interview with Larry Roberts, Monty's brother, 1997:

"First of all, in nineteen forty-eight and nineteen forty-nine, I was riding and showing a horse called Oriole. We didn't have a horse called Oriel, so I assume Monty is referring to my horse as having been the one with him in the desert, and that's just impossible.

"Oriole was with me and we sure weren't with Monty in Nevada. We were at horse shows nearly every weekend or at the rodeo grounds. Monty

and Brownie were there too. We were all in California, right around Salinas."

The Man Who Listens to Horses:

> For the next three years ['49, '50, '51] I would be crossing the Sierra Nevada . . . to live alongside wild herds for several weeks at a time. (p.6)

> For the next two summers ['50, '51], I would round up mustangs for the Salinas rodeo . . . . (p.21)

An article in a 1950 edition of the local newspaper chronicles and credits well-known stock contractor Harry Rowell as the person who furnished mustangs to Salinas for the wild horse race at the rodeo that year.[10] Likewise, on June 11, 1951, an article on the front page of the *Salinas Californian* notes that two truckloads of wild horses had been delivered to the rodeo grounds for the wild horse races. The article said they were the property of Cuff Burrell, one of the shows stock suppliers. There is no mention of Monty Roberts in either article.

Monty's attendance records show that he did not miss one day of school during the 1948–1949 school year. School wasn't out for summer vacation until the first week of June, and the rodeo was held the third week of June. When could he have spent three weeks with the mustangs that arrived in Salinas at least two weeks prior to the show?

When questioned in 1998, by a doubtful journalist, about his sojourns to Nevada, Monty answered with a

---

[10] *Salinas Californian*, (June 20, 1950).

question of his own, "What difference does it make where I learned *[what I learned from the wild horses]* if in fact, I can do it?"[11]

The Man Who Listens to Horses:

From that experience [with the mustangs in Nevada] I would begin to learn a language, a silent language which I have subsequently termed "Equus." With that as a springboard, I would assemble a framework of ideas and principles that would guide my life's work with horses. I would have none of this were it not for my time as a teenager in the company of mustangs. (p.6)

WILD MUSTANGS & TALL TALES

In the introduction to *The Man Who Listens to Horses,* Lawrence Scanlan asks, "What if Monty had not had the chance to study wild horses?" In actuality, he didn't study horses in the wild as a teenager.

Monty has convinced millions that he spent three summers alone in the high desert of Nevada, learning the language of horses. Research, interviews, and historical documentation belie Monty's claim. Physical evidence and personal testimonials show he did not spend weeks, or even a day, watching wild mustangs in the Nevada desert when he was a teenager.

None of the people associated with Monty during those years believe he went to Nevada. Is that important? Should this memory flaw be ignored?

When asked about the discrepancy between the United Kingdom and United States versions of his book, Monty answered that after the first printings he was

[11] Ronna Snyder, "Horse Whispers—Or Horse Feathers:" *Horse and Rider,"* (February, 1999, P.59)

reminded that it was Ralph and Vivian who were with him.[12] He *forgot?*

RALPH AND VIVIAN CARTER

Carolyn Warner Tugle lived with Ralph and Vivian Carter for nearly two years in the mid-1950s. Carolyn said the joy of being with them was listening to the wonderful stories they told of their lives with horses. She heard tales of horse shows, camping trips, and fun times with the Roberts family. Night after night, they regaled her with horsey vignettes. Some stories she heard more than once. Never though, did she hear a word about a trip to Nevada to round up wild horses with Monty.

According to the memories of everyone at the stables or involved with the rodeo, the wild horses came to the rodeo grounds a few weeks prior to the rodeo and were always sold at auction on the Monday following the rodeo. Neither Larry, nor any of the students at the rodeo grounds, can recall Monty, or anyone else, working or gentling those horses. There are no rodeo association records of any business transaction with Monty Roberts or his brother Larry.

Monty could not have been in Nevada, as he claims, in 1948, 1949, or 1950. The rodeo was also held in June, not July, for those three years. The horses arrived at least three weeks ahead of time. Monty didn't miss school—which didn't get out for summer vacation until the first week of June. The Salinas Junior Rodeo was held in May, and Monty was always a contestant. There are newspaper clippings, horse show programs, photographs, and other items of evidence that place Monty in

[12] Eric Brazil, "Bio called unbridled fiction," *San Francisco Examiner*, (January 11, 1998, Section A, P.1, 18).

Salinas for several weekends in May and June from 1948 through 1952.

Most important of all, there were many, many people around the Roberts family on a daily basis during those years, and all of them insist that Monty was in Salinas at the time in question.

Interview with Ray Roberts, Marvin's brother, 1998:

"Our pride of Monty's accomplishments ended when we read his book.

"My nephew wrote that I was raised by the Cherokee Indians and passed on what I learned about their ways to him. As I said, this is malarkey. Anything Monty learned about horses he learned from his father or on his own.

"As far as I know, he never went on any expedition to Nevada to gather wild horses, and he never spent summers there observing them."

Interview with Dick Gillott, Monty's childhood friend, 1998:

"I just can't figure out how Monty can say the things that he says in that book of his and get away with it. It simply is not the truth. Not the way I remember it. It's not even close to the truth.

"The way I understand it, Monty claims he wanted to find a way to start young horses that wasn't cruel [to them]. He claims his father's methods of breaking a horse were cruel.

"First of all, I don't ever remember Marvin beating or being cruel to a horse. In my opinion, his training methods were never cruel. He did tie a leg up and he did sack them out, but the leg

was tied to keep the horse from hurting himself; it was held just a few inches off the ground, and the sacking out was about the same as having a light sheet tossed at you. It was done to teach the horse that the human was not going to hurt him.

"I was around Marvin and Monty all the time when I was a kid. I never saw or suspected Marvin of being cruel to any horse or to Monty.

"As for Monty's supposed travels in a boxcar to the show horses, I have no explanation. He claims that my brother, Wendell, went with him as a [horse] groom, and I just know that isn't true. Does [Monty] think we are all senile or something?"

Interview with Steve Dorrance, Son of Bill Dorrance, 1998:

"After [my dad said that he wouldn't read past the first sixty pages of Monty's book], I decided to have a look at it myself. My perspective may be different, but from what I saw, his book is all about marketing.

"I've noted that Monty covers most of the current hot topics and finds ways to make them work to his advantage. For instance, he is big on nutrients and health, letting us know that he believes in food supplements and good nutrition. He has mentors. He learned at an early age to set goals and work diligently toward them. He claims to have been physically abused. He claims his father directly caused the death of a Black man and was a racist. I'm sure that if I continue to read, I'll come upon some form of psychotherapy *he needed to recover from the abuse inflicted by his father.*

"In my opinion only, Monty Roberts is one of the most reprehensible people anyone would want to be around. Neither my dad, nor my uncle [Tom Dorrance] ever recall working with Monty or talking to him about his training methods or theirs. Though my dad is in his nineties, he is still very sharp and his memory and faculties are clear.

"A while back, Monty called and requested a photograph of my dad, which was sent, but we wondered why Monty wanted it.

"Monty called about a year after The Man Who Listens to Horses, *was published. He invited both Dad and Uncle Tom to a party at his ranch. Neither of them went.*

"My dad thought it was a strange invitation because he hardly knew Monty."

With an engaging smile, it was nearly forty years later that Monty traded his Stetson cowboy hat for a soft tweed cap and began to convince millions of people that these events took place in his life. By Monty's account, his teenage years were triumphant, yet turbulent. His adventures with horses could rival those of Tom Sawyer and Huckleberry Finn.

Monty regales readers with accounts of his days as a Hollywood stunt rider; his long distance travels in a boxcar with a tutor, a groom, and show horses; and his friendship with legendary film star James Dean. Monty tells of his entrepreneurial spirit with accounts of collecting eighty-thousand Coca Cola bottles, conducting horse training clinics as a child, and maintaining straight As in school despite prolonged absences because of his heavy work schedule.

Monty claims he accomplished all this under Marvin's tyrannical rule and abuse. He also claims that Marvin terrorized horses in the same manner. Worse still, he calls Marvin a racist and a killer.

Imagine the anguish these passages brought to the hundreds of people, including his own brother, who read these tales and knew they were false. It is one thing to stretch the truth a bit, or to expand a story in an effort to paint a clear and vivid picture for the reader. It is quite another to fabricate entire characters and scenarios and give them the names of real people, living or dead. To do this, and then label the collection nonfiction, should be a crime. Some say that it is.

Monty claims that he told his life story—the way he remembers it. A spokesperson at Random House said Monty came with impeccable references and that they had no reason to doubt him.

In a court of law, it would be impossible for a jury to award damages to two people who have been dead for almost fifteen years. Monty knows this. It is far easier to defame the dead than the living. It takes no courage.

Chapter 7

REGARDING EQUINE BEHAVIOR

The Man Who Listens to Horses:

> Later that same summer [1949] I witnessed a fight between two stallions. . . . A bachelor clashed with the alpha male of a family group . . . . [They] reared and pawed each other with their hooves, plunged and kicked and bit. It continued for five or six hours . . . . [The loser] finally left and did not return. . . . A vanquished male will often commit a kind of suicide, deliberately seeking the areas where the cats are, almost offering himself. (pp.25,26)

There are few people in the world who can legitimately claim a career of wild horse observation. Robert Vavra is one. He is not only universally recognized as the world's premier photographer of equines, but an expert in horse behavior. He is the author of more than thirty books published in eight languages.

Vavra's classic study of equine behavior in words and pictures, *Such is the Real Nature of Horses*, was featured in *Life* magazine, has been published in six languages and has been in print for almost twenty years. This singular study of how equines relate to one another in the wild, backed up by photographs, has been praised by the world's leading animal behaviorists, including Dr. Jane Goodall, Dr. George B. Schaller, and Dr. Ian Douglas-Hamilton.

When Robert Redford was ready to film the dream sequence of *The Horse Whisperer*, he personally asked Vavra for advice, not only artistic advice, but advice on horse behavior. Also, since it was a Vavra horse image that appeared on the cover of Nicholas Evans' novel, Redford said he wanted to "loop it" by having Vavra also create an image for the movie posters, print ads, and billboards.

Like Monty, Vavra is in his sixties. For over twenty years he has studied primitive equine behavior in Spain, France, Kenya, South Africa, and Tanzania. When asked to describe the many serious horse battles that he has witnessed over the years in the wild, Vavra commented:

Interview with Robert Vavra, Equine author, photographer, behaviorist, 1999:

"During my years of photographing and observing serious horse battles in the wild— excluding young bachelor intermittent skirmishes—I can't recall an intense combat between mature stallions that lasted over two- and-one-half minutes.

"If they are really engaged in uninterrupted serious rearing-biting combat, horses simply don't have the stamina to go at it much longer than that. Regarding your question of whether a wounded horse would commit a kind of suicide by seeking out predators, offering himself to them: even a herbivore that had all of its limbs bitten off would try to squirm away from a predator's scent.

"If you would like another opinion on this, I can phone Dr. Claudia Feh in France, who has intently, and without pause, studied equines for more than twenty years. She is now involved in reintroducing Prizwalskis back into Mongolia,

128

partly sponsored by the National Geographic
Society to whom she, as an equine behaviorist,
was recommended by Dr. [George] Schaller.

"[Dr. Feh] has literally seen hundreds of
serious horse battles in the Camargue and other
places where she has done her research. Her
credentials are impeccable."

Robert Vavra Interview with Claudia Feh, Equine behaviorist, 1999:

"You ask about all of the serious fights that I
have seen among wild horses during the past
twenty years, which I always tried to time with
a stopwatch. The very longest one, timed with a
stopwatch, lasted exactly four minutes. And
horses, wild or otherwise, unwounded or
seriously wounded, do not seek predators, an act
that would be completely contrary to their
nature."

Whether wild stallions fight for three or four minutes or five or six hours may seem relatively immate-
rial. Whether Monty Roberts knows how long they fight
is of great importance.

If Monty's dissertation regarding the behavior of
wild stallions is completely contrary to that of the
world's leading experts, should Monty's other statements about wild horse behavior be taken seriously?
Should he be considered credible? Or is Monty an example of an individual with a vivid imagination and a
large need for glory?

CALIFORNIA HORSEMASTERSHIP COMPETITION

In 1948, Monty, Larry, and Joyce competed in the state champion junior horsemanship contest. They made it to the finals, but failed to win titles. The outcome was very different in 1949 and 1950.

The Man Who Listens to Horses:

[In 1949, Larry and I] were unprepared [for the California horsemastership competition] and came home losers. . . . [In 1950, I was] victorious in the district . . . . [Later, at the state competition] I won, but it was no surprise . . . . (p.87)

In 1949, a few of the students chose to compete in the California Horsemastership Contest for juniors. It was a rigorous statewide competition that culminated in the fall. The records show that the champion junior horseman that year was a thirteen-year-old boy from Monterey County who won with an overall percentage score of better than ninety-nine percent.[13] The winner was Larry Roberts.

The competition was not based solely on horsemanship, but was multifaceted to also test equine knowledge. To understand the honor of winning this title, it is important to look at the competition itself.

California was divided into nine regions comprised of several counties each. The regions then held eliminations and those winners went to the state competition.

At the regional contest, the competitors were grouped for instructions. There would be no conversation between them once competition began.

---

[13] Jack Huber, "Hoof Beats, Orchids for Our Junior Horsemen," *Salinas Californian,* (April 1, 1950, Section A, P.18).

They took a written exam: a test to identify every single piece of Western and English riding equipment. The items in question were spread out and numbered on a table.

Next, competitors were required to name and properly demonstrate the use of grooming equipment. Each phase of the contest had a different judge.

After the grooming equipment, came the saddling and bridling of a horse. Again, this was done with both Western and English equipment.

There followed the examination of four horses that were tied to a fence. Competitors had to name the breed of each animal. Farther down the line were several more horses, and under the supervision of a veterinarian, competitors had to pick out all of the faults and blemishes of each horse. They were then asked to name and locate one hundred different parts of the horse anatomy.

Monty, Joyce, and Larry in 1948. (Photo courtesy of *The Salinas Californian*—Allmond and Parnell photo).

The second phase of the elimination was based on riding skill. The contestants were judged, again by different judges, for their performance on a Western stock horse, their horsemanship in the English saddle, and their ability to ride jumpers.

When the final scores were tallied in 1949, the Roberts did not go home losers as Monty states. The winner—with an amazing score of more than ninety-nine percentage points—was never the favorite.

Larry Roberts hated school and hated to study. His parents told him that his older brother would use the better horses for the competition.[14] They encouraged Larry to enter for the experience, but they never expected him to beat Monty.

Larry Roberts did study. He studied the things he loved. He studied horses and was named the state champion in 1949, winning with a score of almost one hundred percent.

A defeated but determined Monty won the title in 1950 when the finals were held in Palm Springs. Marvin and Marguerite were always proud of their sons. Both earned the title of state champion; both worked hard to earn that title.

The Man Who Listens to Horses:

When I traveled to New York [after winning the state title] to win the final event with points to spare, I was still only fifteen. Nearly all the other twenty finalists were at the maximum age of eighteen. Fifteen of them came from various states in the United States; the rest were from Canada, Mexico, Panama, Puerto Rico, South Africa, and Argentina. (p.87)

---

[14] They felt the older brother had fewer years left to try for the coveted junior title.

In two years, Marvin and Marguerite's sons became two of the best junior horsemen in the state of California. If there had been a national, or international, level contest connected to the state contest, surely Monty would have been entered. However, no such final competition was affiliated with the state contest known as California Horsemastership. Monty never went to New York to compete or win an international competition "with points to spare," when he was a teenager.

Exaggerations aren't often hurtful. Those in this example might be more appropriately called ego-boosting embellishments. It appears they may have even been designed to be obvious exaggerations because from the countries represented there are more than twenty contestants among the twenty finalists.

The junior horsemen ride down Main Street, Barbrara Muller [Fontes] and Marguerite Roberts leading. circa, 1949. (Photo courtesy of Barbara Fontes—Cook's photo)

However, to call his brother a loser in 1949, especially when Larry actually *won* the competition in question, seems mean spirited and demeaning. Or is it just another lie?

Joyce's Memoirs, Marguerite's sister, 1997:

"A high point in my life came when Monty, Larry, Barbara Muller, Ron Stolich, and I studied to compete in the California State Horsemastership competition. This extraordinary event was held for several years in California. Entrants had to excel in both English and Western riding disciplines.

"We were required to identify various breeds of horses, diagnose horses with an illness or blemish, and determine the ages of a number of horses. We had to identify tack and equipment, both English and Western, and know all the parts of the horse's anatomy.

"Marvin was a patient teacher. He tutored us over and over until we were experts. I have two medals from that competition that I still cherish."

Barbara [Muller] Fontes is the same age as Joyce and Monty and she also spent much of her childhood under Marvin and Marguerite's tutelage. Barbara and Joyce were instant friends. Her father passed away when she was very young, and her mother owned and operated the local drug store.

A woman ahead of her time, Barbara's mom was a working mother with a hectic schedule. She depended heavily on the Roberts to help raise Barbara. If not in school, Barbara could be found at the stables. She was an avid horseperson and loved to compete in the horse shows. It was Marvin and Marguerite who helped her become a winner.

From 1947 through 1953, Barbara competed in horse shows with Monty, Larry, and Joyce.

Interview with Barbara Muller Fontes, Roberts student, 1998:

"I rode horses at the rodeo grounds and was trained by Marvin and Marguerite to ride and care for those horses. They [Marvin and Marguerite] were wonderful to me and treated me like a daughter always.

"I have an article written by Si Allmond that appeared in the Tri-County Horseman *in nineteen forty-nine. The article chronicles Larry Roberts' win on Oriole at Pebble Beach that summer and my win of the horsemanship class at the same show. Though the article doesn't mention him, I recall Monty being there with the rest of us. Monty claims to have spent most of that summer in the high desert of Nevada. That is impossible.*

"I was also surprised to read in Monty's book that after winning the state horsemastership contest in Palm Springs, he traveled to New York to win the final event 'with points to spare.'

"I was surprised because I competed with him in Palm Springs, and I know there was no final competition in New York. It was already autumn and we were all back in school. I remember

getting our pictures taken for the front page of the Salinas Californian *after winning at Palm Springs.*

"I also have difficulty comprehending Monty's travels in a retrofit railroad boxcar with his horses and tutor while he showed horses and put on horsemanship clinics and demonstrations.

"It was Marvin and Marguerite who hauled us around in an old blue van. They did what they could, but they were not wealthy. In my wildest imagination, I could not have envisioned the traveling boxcar with advance scouts.

"My memories are not faulty. I do not suffer from any childhood trauma or Alzheimer's disease. I remember clearly and vividly the wonderful days of my youth. I was privileged to ride and show horses with the Roberts."

In the late 1940s and the years that followed, the Roberts home would have been well served by a revolving door at its center. Most of those who contributed to this book spent at least a night or two with the family. Others were in and out of the house on a regular basis, from early in the morning until well past dark. The little red two-bedroom home was the hub of activity around the stables and rodeo grounds.

ANGER?

The Man Who Listens to Horses:
[At my father's funeral] I will not forget the triggers that set [my father] off—when I forgot one

of his orders, or defied him.... [I'd receive] another bloodied skull, another trip to Dr. Murphy. (p.175)

> I knew the triggers that led to violence. I, too, have felt that anger rise in me, felt the urge to strike out at someone in my family. But I put my grip on that anger. I swore that this man in the box would be the last link in the chain of violence and anger aimed as much at humans as at horses. (p.175)

Throughout his book, Monty paints his father as a man prone to anger. It would seem reasonable that such a man could not forever hide this tendency from the people who were around him on a daily basis.

The Roberts did not lead a life behind closed doors. Their home and their hearts were open to all. Many people were recipients of their love and generosity over the years. A majority of their students spent much more than a night or two with the family. Others were with them from early morning until late into the night.

With so many people around their house and stable all of the time, surely someone might have, at the very least, suspected that Marvin was prone to anger as Monty says. Someone might have suspected or known that he possessed a trait or two of those described by Monty. Someone might have suspected or known that he could be cruel or abusive to horses as Monty claims.

Surely not all of these people would be wanting to hide such a terrible thing as Monty describes.

After nearly three years of searching for someone to confirm Monty's allegations against his father, no credible source has been found.

By now, the question may come unbidden: Could Marvin have hidden these traits from his relatives, his

137

best friends, and the others who were around him all the time? Could he have been thoughtful, caring, generous, and loving to everyone but his oldest son, Monty? If so, then Marguerite would also be guilty of hiding her true nature.

Behind her obstreperous alpha female personality and take-charge attitude, did there lurk a meek, subservient woman, whose spirit was subjugated to that of her husband? Did she allow Marvin to beat their child and treat their horses in a cruel manner? Are these *reasonable* possibilities?

A search by family members, friends, several investigative reporters, and a team of attorneys to find a truth based in reality about any anger, abuse, or cruelty in the Roberts family brought a yield of only one name—Monty Roberts.

If there is any link between the Roberts family and violence or anger expressed toward horses or humans—it began with Monty Roberts, not the father on whom he tries to lay the blame.

Interview with Skeeter Garcia Innocenti, Roberts student, 1998:

"I remember Monty as the one with a temper. [It seemed to me] he had no patience with horses. If a horse didn't do what he asked, Monty would often jump down and whip the horse in the face until it was running backwards to get away from him. I saw him do this when he was a teenager.

"One time his horse ran backward into the barn post and [the post] broke in half. That made Monty really mad. I watched him pick up a piece of that broken post and use it on the horse.

138

Wendell the stable hand finally stopped him. It was awful to watch.

"I was shocked. I was younger [than Monty] and had always looked up to him. I knew there was no excuse for what he did to that horse—no excuse for getting angry like that."

Interview with Larry Roberts, Monty's brother, 1998:

"Gilbert Lucero was a friend of ours who rode at the stables and spent a lot of time with us. Gilbert was helping us stack straw in the barn when Monty lost his temper. I still don't know what the fight was about, but Monty was raging mad at Gilbert.

"The next thing I remember was seeing a hay hook fly across the barn. Monty got so mad at Gilbert that he threw a ten-inch hay hook at him. It stuck in the wall right alongside of Gil's head!

"I just froze and watched the whole thing.

"Beek was there too. Gilbert took off running, and Beek ["Beek" is a nickname for Allen Martins] started telling Monty that he had just done a very foolish thing. Beek was staring at Monty, and his eyes were like two big ole black holes in a shotgun barrel. He was as shocked as I was.

"Beek told him it was a really, really stupid thing to do and that he could have killed Gilbert. Then Beek asked Monty if he had any idea how dangerous it had been to throw that hook at Gilbert.

"I guess Gilbert ran and told our father,

because about that time Daddy walked in and straight over to Monty.

"He talked to us for five or ten minutes and made it clear that he didn't want to see this sort of thing happen again, ever. That was pretty much the end of it. I think Monty and Gilbert were both very lucky that day.

"We were teenagers when that happened. I knew a flying hook could kill somebody. Monty and Gilbert knew it too."

Interview with Larry Roberts, Monty's brother, 1997:

"We used to play polo. One day Monty and I were practicing at the far end of the grounds. I was not wearing a helmet. Now I admit, we had been told we had to wear helmets, but I was not wearing mine.

"I remember clearly that the ball was not in play when Monty rode up behind me and swung that mallet. He hit me right in the head and said, 'Dad told you to wear a helmet.'

"Monty split my head open and blood started pouring out. I got scared. I rode Oriole straight to the house, got off, and ran inside.

"Daddy saw the loose horse and came to see what was going on. He took one look at me and said, 'Larry! What happened to you?'

"I told him that Monty hit me with a polo mallet and split my head open.

"I had to go get stitches. They shaved my hair all off to stitch me up. I don't think Monty even got a spanking for that.

"When I got back from the hospital, Monty made fun of how I looked and told me again that I should have been wearing a helmet."

Interview with Allen "Beek" Martins, Monty's uncle, 1997:

"Monty used to throw terrible temper tantrums when he was young. I remember the time he [got angry and] threw a pitchfork at Jim's back [Martins] and it stuck right in him.

"My God, when Jim fell face down, that pitchfork was sticking straight up out of his back! I thought Monty had killed Jim for sure. He easily could have.

"I was also there the day Monty got mad at Gilbert Lucero and threw a hay hook at him. The hook missed Gilbert, and it stuck in the wall of the barn just a few inches from his head."

The Man Who Listens to Horses:

Suddenly [Brownie] felt all wrong beneath me. . . . I knew he was dead. . . . A terrible grief overtook me. (pp.97,98)

Monty writes loving prose about his United States Cavalry remount horse, Brownie. He tells of awards, travels, clinics, and other adventures they shared.

Interview with Larry Roberts, Monty's brother, 1997:

"Brownie was a great horse. He'd do just about anything for Monty. Once, after they won a class, the photographer was trying to get Brownie's ears up for a picture. He put a few rocks in a can and shook it. Brownie spooked and

141

started spinning like crazy with Monty up there—it was the kind of spin that a judge would love to see in a stock horse class.

"Later Monty got some marbles, put them in a can, and practiced using the can to get Brownie to spin. Daddy saw this and reminded Monty that he couldn't take the can in the show ring. He told Monty that Brownie was only spinning like that because he was scared, and he asked Monty not to do it again. That was about the extent of discipline we got from Daddy. He would either ask us to do something, or to not do something. He rarely raised his voice.

"One day Monty was working Brownie out near the catch corrals. He'd been out there for an hour or so when I went in for lunch. When I went back out, Brownie was all lathered up hot and sweaty. I knew they'd been working hard and asked Monty if he didn't think Brownie had had enough.

"Well, that sure started something. Monty got mad so I left him there and went back to the barn. It wasn't long before Monty walked back too—on foot.

"He was crying and said Brownie was dead. The next minute he started talking about how Daddy gave Brownie too much alfalfa. I couldn't believe it. He was blaming Daddy?

"He went and got Mom, and the three of us went out to where he'd left Brownie. The horse still had lather [from sweating] all over him and welts on his butt [whip marks].

"I stood there, staring at Brownie, and thought about how many times Daddy told us not to work our horses too hard without resting them."

ACCIDENTS

Marvin and Marguerite constantly cautioned others to be careful around the horses. The rules they enforced were for the safety of both the students and the horses. Every rule had a reason behind it. One rule was to always tie a horse to a solid post or hitching rail, never to a board rail fence.

Joyce's Memoirs, Marguerite's sister, 1997:

"I was about fifteen when a man brought in a young thoroughbred mare. She had gotten herself tangled in a barbed-wire fence and nearly severed her right front leg at the knee.

"The veterinarian recommended putting the mare down. He said the wound would continue to open because of its location and was unlikely to heal.

"I pleaded with the man to let me take the horse. Marvin cautioned me about the huge responsibility of tending her. He said I should be prepared for a long ordeal of treating the wound several times a day. He did, however, offer to help me if I was committed to saving the mare.

"I assured him I'd do everything possible to get her well. He then mixed his special wound dressing, and we went to work.

"Marvin was the only person other than me that thought the mare had any chance to recover.

Like he predicted, it was a long ordeal. She did recover, and Marvin let me breed her to his quarter horse stallion.

"That mating produced a beautiful colt for me. He is pictured in The Man Who Listens to Horses *with Monty on his back. Monty is receiving a trophy after winning a hackamore class on him in nineteen fifty-two.*

"Shortly after the photo was taken Monty tied him to a board rail fence. I don't know the exact circumstances but the fence broke and my horse ended up with a broken leg."

MR. SALINAS JUNIOR

The Man Who Listens to Horses:
> When I won the "Mr. Salinas Junior" bodybuilding contest, my father ridiculed me. (p.94)

Monty's own words probably describe him best: "I was prone to think I was better than anyone else and that I possessed unique qualities."[15]

The contest was held at the El Rey Theatre. Dick Gillott remembered going to watch. He said that Monty competed and was mad as hell because he didn't win. Gillott said Monty placed in the competition, but he is certain that Monty did not win.

No one else remembers Monty winning this title either.

An ego-boosting whisper. A pretentious little lie.

[15] Monty Roberts, *The Man Who Listens to Horses,* (Random House, 1997)

Chapter 8

1951, Change in the Air

The very subtle changes began in 1951. The boys and girls who were the junior horsemen and women were becoming just that—men and women. They were finding new interests. There was an entire world available beyond the gates of the rodeo grounds, and the three youngsters that had formed the nucleus of the organization were cautiously preparing to ride into unknown territory.

Joyce and Pete fell in love at a rodeo in King City in the spring of 1951. Pete tried to hide his feelings at first, but his pals, Tony Vargas and Ron Koch, said it was obvious to them that he was smitten with Joyce. She was still in high school when they met, but she graduated in June of 1952 and married Pete the following March.

For Joyce, riding and showing horses was a joyous avocation slowly fading into the pages of childhood memories.

Interview with Pete Renebome, Joyce's husband, 1998:

"I left college to work on a ranch in the Ruby Mountains of Nevada. After a long haying season, I had a paycheck in my pocket and a week's vacation coming. It was Labor Day weekend, and we cowboys were looking for a rodeo. We had narrowed the choice to Eureka or Winnemucca. I flipped a coin, and it came up heads. I left for Winnemucca.

"It was at the Winnemucca rodeo that I met Tony Vargas, Ronnie Koch, and Gene Hammon,

all from Salinas. We hit it off, and I told them to call if there was work out their way. In February, Ronnie called to say the Montgomery Ranch was looking for a cowboy. With two feet of snow at the ranch near Jiggs, the Salinas Valley sounded like a good idea.

"I met Joyce a few months later. We were at the fair in King City when I saw her walking with a couple of friends and pestered Ronnie and Tony about her. They said they knew her, and Ronnie made the introductions. She was at the big dance the next night too. I was so bashful that it took me more than an hour to get up my nerve to ask her to dance. Once I did, I didn't want to let her go.

"She introduced me to her sister, Marguerite, who I thought was her mother. I asked Marguerite if Joyce could go to the carnival with me. She gave me a long list of rules, but said yes. Marguerite was loud, clear, and firm in her instructions: no more than one hour, no drinking, no leaving the fairgrounds, and no smoking.

"She delivered her rules in a jovial way, but I knew the message was serious. After that night, I made the hour-long drive to Salinas from the ranch near King City nearly every weekend to visit Joyce. Most of the time I found her at the Roberts. It was like she had two sets of parents.

"Joyce graduated from high school the next year, and we were married the year after that. Not a day has gone by, in more than forty-seven

146

years, that I don't count my blessings the coin came up heads."

Marguerite was a party planner. She loved to organize and orchestrate the myriad of details that went into entertaining. From casual barbecues in the back-yard to elaborate holiday feasts, box socials, association dinners, and intimate engagement parties for fifty or sixty people, Marguerite was an accomplished hostess.

When Joyce confided that Pete Renebome had proposed, Marguerite insisted on a junior horsemen party to celebrate. To accommodate everyone, she booked the banquet room at Walkers Cafe. It was just one example of the wonderful things Marguerite did to make people feel special. Ted and Phyllis Walker were special friends who gave the couple all the Chateau Napoleon champagne for their wedding.

The celebration of a new beginning for Joyce and Pete also forged the end of an era. There had been good times, happy times, but the winds of change were in the air for those who grew up under the spell of the aromatic eucalyptus and the scent of horses at the rodeo grounds. The children were no longer children.

1951, A New Generation Learns to Ride

When Marilyn Albertson Cole's father realized his daughter was not about to lose her love of horses, despite a concussion and a lot of bumps and bruises, he took her to Marvin and Marguerite so she could learn from the best. The year was 1951.

Interview with Marilyn Albertson Cole, Roberts student, 1998:

"I thank the Lord that my parents were able

to do so much for me. When I was a young girl, I wanted a horse more than anything.

"Not knowing where to start, my dad bought a stallion that had been used for roping. Dad and I were both injured when we were bucked off while riding double one day. I ended up with a concussion, and Dad decided to let me ride with the Roberts.

"Marguerite used to pick me up every day from high school. I loved going there. The Roberts were so good to us we never wanted to leave. Sometimes I'd get to stay and have dinner with them too. Being around them was wonderful. They had a way of always making me feel good about myself.

"Thinking back, I have to say that Marvin and Marguerite demanded respect from their students, and that respect grew to love. They helped shape our lives. As a student, they were always there for me. I was never famous as a rider but certainly won my share of ribbons and trophies. My parents were busy and, though they gave me everything, they didn't have the horse knowledge to be my mentors or help me with my passion for horses. Marvin and Marguerite were there for that. They took me to the horse shows, made sure I was prepared, encouraged me to do my best, and applauded me whether I won or lost.

"The Roberts gave me much more than riding lessons and a box full of trophies and ribbons;

they gave me a solid foundation on which to build my life."

Interview with Chet Moore, Roberts student, 1998:

"We moved to Salinas in nineteen forty-six and my parents, like so many others, set about reestablishing their lives after the war. By nineteen forty-nine, they thought my brother John and I should learn to ride. I suspect it was a parental plot designed to keep two rambunctious boys separated in the afternoons. John would go to the rodeo grounds one day, and I would go the next.

"We learned to ride on Boots and eventually got a wonderful and patient horse of our own, complete with Garcia saddle and all the tack. At the horse shows, John and I were in different age groups. Out he would come from his class, we'd drop the stirrups, and back in I would go.

"We were also active in the junior horsemen's association and I remember the leadership experience of being the president one year. As so many others, we were in large part raised under Marvin and Marguerite's watchful eyes. At the rodeo grounds, we learned far more than horsemanship from Marvin and Marguerite Roberts.

"Not the book learning variety, but of values. We learned of truth, of being responsible for our own actions, and of being honest. Along the way, we learned a few other things.

"We learned that a hay barn was not

149

necessarily used only for the storage of hay. (And therefore was off limits!) We learned to dust off and get back on if we were thrown, to keep riding, not to give up, and not to quit. Marvin and Marguerite were for so many of us surrogate parents. It is inconceivable to me that Monty's claims have one scintilla of truth.

"For a son to defame his long dead parents is bad enough. For a son to reap unimaginable profit from such despicable conduct must mark the nadir of the human experience. Monty Roberts has provided me with new meaning to the word 'dishonorable.'"

A LEGACY

Even the best equestrian cannot win, nor accomplish his task well, without a good, well-trained horse. Unlike a machine, the rider cannot simply push a button and cause the horse to perform in a certain manner. Whether that horse is used for working on a ranch, pulling a carriage, or performing in the show arena, he is a full participant and partner with his rider or handler.

The bond that forms between horse and rider, when both are trained and prepared, is the magic epoxy that Marvin Roberts used to create win-win relationships between students and horses. A horse is a living, breathing, beautiful animal that has coexisted and worked side by side with the human animal for thousands of years.

Throughout history, the horse has aided humankind. Often misunderstood, this noble creature has carried us to victory, plowed our fields, and helped settle continents. Anyone who knows the pleasure of owning or caring for a horse that is a willing partner, knows of this unique bond and interdependence.

"Don't just sit up there. I want to see you become one with your horse!" Marguerite used to admonish her students from the center of the ring.

Whether a child or an adult, no matter how much a human feels an emotional connection with a horse, the first actual ride on a horse can be traumatic. It's all about confidence. Marvin knew this and never made a student feel bad or inferior because of fear.

It didn't matter if the student was four years old or fourteen, Marvin would ride along behind them until they were confident on their own. Most of his students can remember that special little half-saddle he had made to fit against the cantle of the student's saddle. It was a lightweight, little pad of a seat with iron stirrups much like that of a jockey's flat saddle, without a pommel, or front, of any kind. He didn't use it often. But when fear overcame desire, Marvin would bring it out to assure the future horseperson that he'd be right there with them. It seldom took long. Having Marvin there was like having training wheels. He was there if needed and gave the rider confidence. Because he was a large man, the school horses Marvin used for beginners were nearly always part draft horse. Their large size could easily accommodate the child and the trainer.

Most students were riding on their own after a few short lessons with Marvin. By that time, the student had learned several basic riding maneuvers and could begin to communicate with the horse. Perhaps the greatest training aid Marvin employed was the ever dependable school horse.

A master in his field, a school horse taught a rider because the horse knew what to do, even if the rider did not. A good school horse is not born, he is made. His training takes years. He is the new rider's coach, mentor, and confidence builder.

A good school horse has learned not to shy or get skittish when he is surprised. If something goes wrong, as it often does, he will stand and wait for instructions. He has learned to accept the challenge and to work with the human who does not yet fully know how to communicate with him. The school horse is the teacher who will help shape a new rider's life. Without the school horse, the work of Marvin and Marguerite, or anyone else training beginning horsepersons, is difficult. It is the horse who ultimately teaches the most.

Marvin was a master with the school horse. He worked tirelessly to train these valuable assistants.

They Called Him Boots

His name was Boots. With four white stockings and a blazed face, the sorrel gelding was every kid's dream. Barn-sour, kid-wise, school horse that he was, he was unbeatable.

Marvin Roberts bought Boots from a stock dealer at the King City Rodeo. He was a nine-year-old buckin' horse from the string that just didn't buck so well anymore. Always needing extra horses, Marvin figured he could gentle Boots and use him as a school horse. A school horse he became.

No one actually knows the number of aspiring horsemen and women who boarded the back of Boots at one time or another. They surely number in the hundreds. He never bucked or ran away with anyone. He'd baby-sit the youngest little girl, make that thirteen-year-old buckaroo feel like Roy Rogers, and give a future rodeo queen the confidence she needed, all in a day's work. A little hay, a few oats, a rubdown, and the day was over.

Boots was never meant for fame or fortune. The old gelding earned his keep, did his job, and got into trouble when he didn't want to leave the barn on a hot day. Few who rode him will ever forget him.

As the children that rode him got older, so did Boots. He'd drop a lead now and then. His pace slowed considerably. Other school horses now had more fire and pizzazz. There were some three- and four-year-old kids who still thought Boots was terrific. He was.

Boots remained with the Roberts until his death; around 1968 is as near as anyone can recollect.

If a love affair with horses begins while riding a school horse, it only deepens after riding a champion.

SIGNIFICANCE

Jack Huber, President of the Monterey County Horsemen's Association, said in 1950, "I don't believe you can find a single case on record in your juvenile courts here in Salinas of any juvenile delinquent who has ever owned or had horses as a hobby. This is no isolated case, but one that is quite prevalent throughout the country."

There are scores of books available on child rearing, and there are scores of books about horses. From teaching toddlers and communicating with wild mustangs to winning at work and riding a champion, the books have been written. There are books to keep children out of trouble and books to correct a horse's bad habits. Books bought by people trying to find an answer. In two sentences, Jack's words, uttered nearly fifty years ago, might well be providential to parents in the coming millennium.

"To a horse-crazy nine-year-old girl, the world of Marvin and Marguerite Roberts at the California Rodeo Grounds in Salinas was as close to heaven as it was possible to get. I had a love affair with horses that started as far back as I can remember. My parents finally said we would look for a horse, and I was ecstatic.

"It did not take long to find the horse of my dreams at the Roberts. He was a red roan with white markings and a beautiful head. Best of all, he had a lot of fire! I was nine and thought he was fast, powerful, and wonderful. Marguerite picked me up every day after school, except Monday, and I rode to my heart's delight. On Saturday, I spent the whole day at the rodeo grounds. I had a wonderful time, and Marvin and Marguerite were my personal heroes. There were a lot of us who rode with the Roberts [during the nineteen fifties]. We had matching chinks [leather chaps cropped below the knee to protect a riders legs from brush, ropes, etc.], shirts, and hats, and [we] paraded very seriously down Main Street during the California Rodeo. Sometimes one of us would be lucky enough to be chosen the 'Best Appearing Boy or Girl' for the day and win extra prizes.

"Marvin had a few racehorses, and I loved to watch the horses work around the track and hounded him with questions. He always had time for me and was one of the kindest men to this day that I have ever met. Besides all the horse

activity, Marvin was a policeman, and I knew him! I was always especially proud as he greeted me each day when he took us across Main Street on our way to Washington Junior High School. This was very important to a girl of eleven.

"It wasn't long before I wanted to compete in junior rodeos and horse shows. In nineteen fifty, most junior classes were for ages eighteen and under. Since my horse was a bit too hyper[active] for the monotonous classes like pleasure and horsemanship, we concentrated on gymkhana events. My favorite was always musical chairs. I learned quickly that when others were eliminated and the race was down to the final two contestants, the winner needed maneuverability, speed, and a horse that stopped quickly. My horse had a lot of speed, but not a lot of whoa.

"My parents dutifully went to the junior rodeos to watch me compete. They watched me in the gymkhana events, and they watched the other students show in the more prestigious classes that I thought were boring. It didn't take long for them to decide I should compete in other events. Marvin and Marguerite were given the task of finding a suitable horse for me. Given the opportunity, I wanted to show in the stockhorse event. Even back then, a decent stockhorse was expensive, and one-thousand dollars was needed to come up with anything competitive that a twelve-year-old could ride.

"I had to buy this horse with my baby-sitting

money, and I only had two hundred and fifty dollars. Undaunted, the Roberts continued to look for a horse for me. They found a four-year-old white mare that worked cattle well, could slide, spin, and was gentle. The only catch was that she would cost four hundred dollars.

"Ralph and Vivian Carter had the mare and were willing to take my wonderful horse, Peanuts, in on trade for the extra hundred and fifty dollars. This seemed like a great solution to everyone but me. I could not bear to give up my first horse.

"Somehow, my mother came up with the extra money for the white mare we called Cricket. I was now the proud owner of two horses.

"Cricket was a beautiful mare with a long and wavy mane and tail. She was very white, and it took a lot of bedding to keep her in that condition. I noticed when I gave her a bath that she had black spots under her hair. Once in a while she would get black hairs in her mane and tail, and I would pull them out because I wanted her to be snow white. Cricket had a smooth gait, and she was perfect for the Western medal classes. Marvin and Marguerite spent hours helping me become a better rider. When it was time to go to the shows, they would use the horse van and, if necessary, Marguerite would haul a horse trailer behind her station wagon, and we were off to the weekend shows. I didn't just ride horses with the Roberts, I stayed many weekends at their house. I'm not sure why they put up with me so much,

156

but I was very happy to have the wonderful opportunity to spend so much time with them.

"Naturally, with a new horse, I needed a show saddle and the Roberts saw to it that I had nothing but the best. Henry and Angie Garcia had a beautiful saddle made just for me. It fit me and my horse perfectly, and I still use it many times a week [forty years later].

"I started showing at [small local shows] and progressed from there. We even traveled a couple of hours north to Woodside and to the Cow Palace in San Francisco.

"I loved the horse show and rodeo world. Roping especially fascinated me as did cutting and working cow horses. Because of Marvin and Marguerite, I was exposed to all these different activities.

"After graduating from high school, I had Cricket bred to a distinguished local quarter horse stallion. I didn't know much about the different breeds of horses then but thought my mare was a cross between an Arabian and a Morgan. She wasn't too tall, yet she was very broad. I worried about color. The stallion was a bay. Imagine my surprise when I found a beautiful Appaloosa foal standing at her side!

"He was a beautiful bay with a white blanket over his rump, dotted with the characteristic Appaloosa spots. I took pictures and rushed over to tell the Roberts. My life continued to revolve around horses, in a slightly different way.

"Watching the colt grow, I knew he was

exceptional. I took him to the state fair and showed him in the halter class against thirty-two [other yearlings]. He placed second. That's when Myrtle and Ed Brown wanted to know about the breeding of my colt. I named the sire and said I thought my mare was a Morab.

"Together they said, 'Impossible!' One of the parents had to be an Appaloosa to get an Appaloosa. They told me I had a quality colt, and I should determine Cricket's breeding. Back to Marvin and Marguerite I went to try to trace [her] pedigree.

"[We discovered] she was indeed an Appaloosa. Her sire was a thoroughbred named Bayards Son by Bayards Two out of El Mirasol. With more research, I learned that Bayards Son's great, great-grandfather, Ben Brush, won the Kentucky Derby in eighteen ninety-six.

"I became very interested in Appaloosa horses and bred my mare, Chans Royal Cricket, twelve times to Tripe-A quarter horses or stakes winning thoroughbreds. She was never bred to an Appaloosa. From those unions, she produced twelve good-looking, colored foals for me. All the while she was used as a show and rodeo horse. As my children grew up, they rode Cricket to many wins with Marvin and Marguerite guiding them. Sherri, my daughter, won her first trophy riding by herself on Cricket at nineteen-months-

old. It was in the Small Fry class at the Monterey County Junior Rodeo. [16]

"Over these many years, my husband, Henning Koch, and I have won countless awards on the sons and daughters of Cricket. One year, a colt was born that we elected to keep as a stallion. His sire was an outstanding quarter horse known as Sugar Bars. We named our colt Double or Nothin', and he had a major career in halter, racing, show, rodeo, and even endurance riding. He did it all, and he did it well.

"We showed him all over the country, traveling as far east as Kentucky, and we even took him to Canada for the prestigious Appaloosa National Show where he was named the overall High Point Horse of the show.

"Double's lifetime career is incredible. He was one of the first Appaloosa's to run triple-A. We raced him as a two-year-old in New Mexico, Colorado, and Texas. He was the third-ranked two-year-old colt in the nation in nineteen seventy-two. When he came back from the track, we gave him a year off, only showing him in eight halter shows, including the Cow Palace where he won his class. At the same show, along with his three-quarter brother, he won a Produce of Dam class for Cricket. As a four-year-old, we only rode him at our ranch and waited until he was five to begin showing him in California.

---

[16]A classic example of the Roberts legacy, Suzanne's story continues far beyond 1950. That story is shared here as a glimpse of the remarkable longevity of Marvin and Marguerite's impact.

"We used the knowledge passed to me by Marvin and Marguerite throughout our training and care of this great stallion. He performed well because we worked together as a team. He was not taught to fear man and was never abused. Once we started showing him again, his credits and titles continued to grow.

"We successfully competed in working cow horse, cutting, poles, barrels, pleasure, matched pairs, team roping, calf roping, and anything else that looked like fun. He was my Women's Professional Rodeo Association mount at the rodeos in barrel racing. When he was ten, we took him competitive trail riding, and he excelled in that as well. He won his medallion in that event in less than two and one-half months. On his first ride with one hundred and seventeen horses competing, he came in fifth!

"You see, it is not just in my mind that I learned so much from Marvin and Marguerite. Double or Nothin' is a direct product of their legacy: not a horse that performs out of fear, but a horse who loves to work with humans.

"We have bred many nice mares to this fine stallion over the years and still ride his foals. His last foal crop is coming three in nineteen ninety-eight. Sadly, he died three years ago and is now buried on our ranch. He is resting next to his mother, Cricket, and her first foal, Sparkette. Cricket lived to be thirty-two, Sparkette twenty-eight, and Double or Nothin' twenty-five.

"My love of horses and horse shows has never

waned. We have been doing a lot of cutting and have a nice mare named Dubs Jewel. She is out of an Ima Freckles Too mare by Double or Nothin'. Jewel won the [national title] in Junior Cutting in her four-year-old year and won the [national title] in Senior Cutting as a five-year-old. In nineteen ninety-seven, when she was six, we began to show her in open cuttings. We took her to Carmel Valley Ranchero Days where she won the fifteen hundred class and the three thousand class. An incredible feat for a highly colored Appaloosa in competition with tough quarter horses under a quarter horse judge. We were very proud of her.

"I have been doing a lot of barrel racing again, both in associations and at rodeos. I am riding daughters and sons of Double or Nothin', and they are terrific. Our daughter, Sherri, shows extensively and belongs to the Women's Professional Rodeo Association where she ropes calves, team ropes, goat ties, steer undecorates, and barrel races. She rides Double or Nothin' horses exclusively. In nineteen ninety-five, she won the High Point Non-Pro at the World Show in Fort Worth. At the San Antonio Livestock Show, in nineteen ninety-eight, she won High Point Rider, High Point Cow Horse, High Point Gymkhana Horse, High Point English Horse, and High Point Non-Pro. For this, she received two saddles and five buckles. Sherri also won the Women's Professional Rodeo Association calf roping finals at the Lazy E Arena (three calf

average) on her horse Dubs Charge. She was the Women's Professional Rodeo Association World Champion in the goat-tying event a few years ago. All of these awards were garnered while riding grandsons or granddaughters of my beloved Cricket.

"George Hatley of the Appaloosa Horse Club said that Cricket was the premiere dam in the Appaloosa world. We were recently notified that Double or Nothin' has been inducted into the [Appaloosa] National Hall of Fame.

"Marvin and Marguerite Roberts took a little girl and made all her dreams come true. I gratefully accepted their understanding, patience, coaching, and good spirits. Nothing was better than to do a good job at a horse show and to have them praise me. My dreams are still coming true today thanks to the Roberts. In my opinion, there were no better people anywhere in the world. They are still my heroes."

Sherri Mell with Dubs Charge, Rosie, and Wild Willy Bar at the San Antonio Livestock Expo, February 1998. (Courtesy of Suzanne Koch, Shirley photo).

What if a student didn't win? What if the blue ribbon went to someone else? What if a student simply wanted to ride her horse and not be bothered to show at all? How did the Roberts react under those circumstances? Did the coaches pay attention to those who would never be superstars?

Interview with Dee Dee Garcia White, Roberts student, 1998:

"I know Marvin and Marguerite did not give lessons just so their students and horses would end up in the winner's circle. They wanted their students to enjoy animals as much as they did. Don't get me wrong, winning was important, but many of their students never entered a show ring. The Roberts devoted equal time to all.

"Marvin taught his students to ride horses, but he did more than that. He built self-esteem and self-confidence while he helped horse and rider understand each other.

"I spent years learning from Marvin and Marguerite. They gave lessons. They did not scream and curse at me. They taught me to be gentle with my hands and not to jerk my horse around.

"When I was seventeen I took a riding lesson from a well-known trainer in Southern California. The lesson lasted less than half an hour. When the trainer started screaming and cursing at me, I got off my horse and walked out of the ring.

"I went on to train horses and give riding

163

lessons in Reno, Nevada, using the methods I learned from Marvin and Marguerite. My horses and students won many state championships, and we owe that success to the Roberts."

Interview with Sandy Sans Rose, Roberts student, 1998:
"I rode with Marvin and Marguerite for several years and always considered them with the highest regard. They were wonderful people. They were patient and kind, and I never once saw Marvin be cruel to a horse. My parents often left me there from daylight until dark. Marvin and Marguerite never complained or charged extra for all the work they put into me and my horse the year I won the All County Cowgirl title. I would not have achieved that honor without them.

"Monty's book will never change my fond memories of them. I think all of us that rode with them thought of them as our second parents."

ROLE MODEL

From countless interviews with everyone close to the Roberts family, comes one clear and vivid portrait: Marvin was a role model.

NEVER, did anyone, EVER, hear Marvin raise his voice in anger or see him raise a hand in violence toward his wife, children, horses, or any other living thing.

Child abuse and battered wives were not often discussed openly in the 1940s and 1950s, but the stories were whispered about individuals who were suspected of this.

Rumors about cruel horse trainers circulated among horse enthusiasts as well. Stories were told of cruel trainers who thought they might force an animal to perform out of fear. There was no shortage of abusive and cruel people in that era, as there is no shortage of them now.

Marvin Roberts was not one of those people. Marvin was gentle, kind, caring, and probably most of all, he was compassionate. He had a way of always making a person feel special. He did the same with horses.

Chapter 9

1953, Thanksgiving Day, November 26

Joyce's Memoirs, 1998:

"Marvin and Marguerite took control when I was in labor with Debra. My daughter, like me, was born on Thanksgiving Day. The year was nineteen fifty-three.

"Pete and I had driven to Salinas from our home in Redwood City, near San Francisco. We were at my parents' house for the traditional family Thanksgiving Day gathering, when I realized that I was having labor pains.

"This was a new experience for Pete and me, but Mom was very casual about it. She didn't seem concerned at all, but told me I might miss dinner.

"I called my doctor and told him to expect me. Next, I called Marguerite.

"Dinner was several hours away, and Flick suggested we stop by her house before going to the hospital. She said I could rest on the couch, and I'd be more comfortable than in the hospital all day.

"She rationalized to me that the first one usually takes a long time to make an appearance. It sounded like a good idea to us.

"Pete and I had everything packed in anticipation and arrived at the rodeo grounds *about fifteen minutes later. Marvin was standing outside waiting for us.*

"He made a big fuss over me, making sure I was as comfortable as possible. He'd gotten out blankets and pillows and even had a hot toddy ready for me.

"He was trying to distract me from the pain with his running commentary about the Thanksgiving Day parade on television. I remember smiling at my sister while Pete held my hand and Marvin fussed. She laughed and said, 'You think this is something, you should have seen him when the boys were born!'

"After a couple of hours we got a frantic telephone call from Dr. [Norman P.] Andresen who had been looking for me all over town! Everyone was so concerned about me that we overlooked calling the doctor back to tell him I'd be coming in later.

"Marvin and Marguerite went to the hospital with us then. Pete and I were grateful. They kept us company and reassured us all would be fine. It meant they were late for Thanksgiving Day dinner, but it meant the world to us.

"After they had dinner, and we had a baby girl, they returned with a piece of my favorite dessert, mayonnaise cake. It was divine."

1954–1955, *East of Eden*

In 1954, Dwight David Eisenhower was president, gasoline sold for twenty-nine cents a gallon, nineteen-inch black-and-white television sets cost nearly two hundred dollars, and U.S. taxpayers paid as much as eighty-seven percent of their income to the Internal Revenue Service.

In Salinas, farming operations were expanding as fields of mustard and native pastures were cleared, the dark, rich soil tilled and furrowed. Row upon ramrod-straight row of lettuce, beans, and beets were planted by wealthy produce farmers with Salinas Valley soil beneath their fingernails and bank accounts as healthy as the food they produced to feed the nation.

Tractors sought to carve more of the valley into a patchwork miasma of crops, and farmers sold their original holdings to developers who covered God's garden with concrete and asphalt. The city was expanding.

A farmer could get much more than he had paid for his land if he sold it for housing. He reasoned he could expand out from the city, and it would not affect his bottom line. If anything, he could become wealthy beyond his dreams of yesteryear.

In 1954, the people of Salinas were full of dreams and desires. Those who had suffered and struggled in poverty were moving ahead. There was money to be made. A new middle class was emerging. Couples drank highballs of bourbon whiskey mixed with water or Seven-Up in tall glasses at cocktail parties, everyone smoked cigarettes, and the men chewed tobacco. Roger Bannister, in England, broke the four-minute mile. It seemed there was nothing to stop them. Life was good.

Early in June of 1954, Elia Kazan and James Dean arrived in Salinas to shoot a few location scenes for the film *East of Eden* from the book written by acclaimed local author John Steinbeck.

Marvin Roberts had the largest stable of horses in the area, and he was asked to supply horses, wagons, and the names of those who might want to be extras on the set.

It was an exciting time around Salinas. Having any connection to a Hollywood film production, no matter how tenuous, seemed glamorous. A link to the movie came with bragging rights and a license to exaggerate. Within days, half the population of Salinas claimed to be under Kazan's direction. Celebrity status was contagious.

The company arrived on June 2 and left on June 11. Most of the film had already been shot in Mendocino, a coastal city north of San Francisco, but the Salinas location was needed to show the vast lettuce fields.

Marvin drove a wagon in one scene, but is hardly recognizable with his hat pulled low. Monty's role in the film is unmistakable, albeit brief. He can clearly be seen loading lettuce with the star, James Dean.

The connection—a brief encounter between a young man who would become an immortal idol and another who yearned for that glory—lends credence to tales of a pretentious relationship that never existed.

The Man Who Listens to Horses:

> Our old friend Don Page was the first assistant director on the film and he suggested that I take this young, unknown actor under my wing . . . let him live with me . . . . there was a $2,500 payment for the three months, plus food allowances . . . . I gave him the top bunk. (pp.101, 102)

> After the three months were up, Don Page and Elia Kazan called me in for a meeting. They . . . wanted to know how their young prospect had fared. (p.103)

I was the wrangler looking after the horses my father had provided . . . [I was] a stuntman and an extra. . . . [I was asked to attend the dailies. Kazan and Page] wanted me to comment on the authenticity of all aspects of the film. (p.103)

[A year later, Dean wanted to] buy a ranch that Pat and I would manage . . . Pat and I felt our future was decided . . . . On September 30, 1955, we were waiting for [Dean's] telephone call. [Dean's] mechanic, Wolf Weutherich, had our names and telephone numbers . . . when [Dean's] Porsche collided with another car. . . . James Dean died of a broken neck. . . . the first call [Weutherich] made was to us. (p.104)

Monty claims he was to be paid twenty-five hundred dollars, plus food allowances, to take James Dean under his wing, let him live in the Roberts household prior to filming, and help him absorb the local atmosphere for three months prior to filming. According to Monty, when the three months were up, Don Page and Elia Kazan called on Monty, then nineteen years of age, to learn how Dean had fared.

When the filming started two days later, Monty says he was asked to attend the dailies and comment on the film's authenticity. He claims that he was an environmental consultant, a wrangler, a stuntman, and an extra for the film.

A little whisper? A little lie?

If Dean spent three months living with the Roberts—where did Larry sleep? Why didn't Larry know James Dean was in the two-bedroom house? How is it that no one else saw a shadow of the actor at the Roberts home?

Monty says that he originally met Don Page in 1939, when Don worked for Warner Brothers, and that Don was the person who suggested Monty for the role as a child stunt double. But Don was actually an actor going by the name Dan Alvarado at that time and did not work in any administrative capacity then for Warner Brothers. In 1941, Don moved to Arizona where he ran a ranch for Jack Warner for the next seven years.

In 1954, Don Page became the first assistant director to Elia Kazan for the filming of *East of Eden*. Kazan had gone to New York, and there he hired James Dean to star in the film. He sent Dean to meet with John Steinbeck who also lived in New York at the time. Steinbeck told Kazan that he didn't like Dean.

Kazan told Steinbeck that he didn't like him either, but that he was perfect for the part of Cal Trask. Steinbeck agreed. From that time on, Dean's life has been documented almost daily. No record can be found to substantiate Monty's claim that James Dean spent time living in the Roberts household in Salinas.

Interview with Tony Vargas, 1998:

"It's interesting that Monty thinks James Dean lived with him for three months prior to the filming of East of Eden. *Dean may well have been friendly toward Monty, but [James Dean] never lived with the Roberts at all."*

Interview with Larry Roberts, 1998:

"I'm still wondering where I was supposed to be when James Dean was sleeping in my bed. It was only a twin!"

Marsha Lacey was away at college, but her friend Monty wrote often to keep her informed of local events. Having ridden at the rodeo grounds from 1948 to 1953, Marsha missed the activity and excitement of the stable.

She read with delight his passages about *East of Eden*. "Dad provided the horses for the film," wrote Monty. "You'll be able to spot some of us [loading lettuce]."

Marsha said that in his letters Monty never mentioned a relationship with any of the actors.

Interview with Skeeter Garcia Innocenti: 1998:

"I remember the filming of East of Eden *well. James Dean and the cast stayed [downtown]. It was exciting to have celebrities around. We all felt important because they used Marvin's horses and our friends were [on the set].*

"Marvin drove a wagon with his black lab Ida up there with him. Marvin kept his head down so he's hard to recognize, but Monty is very visible. He's at the top of the chute loading lettuce, and the camera was on him for maybe fifteen seconds."

Monty's claim that Weutherich called him after the crash, is equally preposterous. Weutherich's jaw was broken; Monty was supposed to be away at college on that Friday; and Monty's wife, Pat, is the only person found to back his story.

Monty also claims to have been with Dean during the filming of *Rebel Without a Cause* and *Giant*. Exhaus-

tive investigative efforts found no one connected to any
of the three films who could recall Monty.

FOOTBALL

The Man Who Listens to Horses:

In 1955 I won a football scholarship . . . . The
"full-ride" scholarship meant that both tuition and
living expenses were paid for. However . . . I
declined the scholarship . . . (p.105)

Interview with Larry Roberts, 1998:

*"Monty played for Hartnell Junior College. I
don't remember that he was ever first string, but
he usually got to play by the last quarter.
Hartnell had a good team that year. I know
Monty went to Pasedena with them for a
championship game.*

*"Monty always seemed to be in the right place
at the right time. Like on the championship-
bound bus for a photo.*

*"Daddy was all in favor of our playing football.
I remember him telling us that, 'It's not
[important] that you get to play in every game.
Keep working hard. You're learning teamwork
and discipline.' He always tried to make us feel
good about ourselves.*

*"Monty and I weren't able to compete in a lot
of different sporting activities like some kids,
because we did have a lot to do at home with our
horses.*

"I never heard anything about my brother winning a football scholarship."

Interview with Angie Garcia, 1998:

"Henry and I used to go everywhere with Marvin and Marguerite. We went with them a lot to watch the boys play football. Larry was a very good [football] player. We watched him all through high school. After that, he went to play for the Navy.

"Monty didn't get to play so much. He usually only played at the very end of the game. Marguerite never said anything to me about Monty getting a football scholarship. I sure would have been surprised.

"Monty wasn't that good at football. Who would offer a scholarship? If he had won that I think Marguerite would have told me."

1955, GROWN UP

Joyce was married with a new baby. Monty had graduated from high school and was making plans for college, more horse shows, and a life with his sweetheart, Pat. Larry was a star athlete, a senior in high school, and planning to play football for the United States Navy when he graduated in 1955.

In the meantime, Larry showed horses less frequently and began to attend as many rodeos as his parents would allow. For him, there was new excitement riding bulls. He loved the rough-and-tumble lifestyle of the rodeo cowboy and the thrill of pitting his own skill against that of the clever bulls they rode. The events in

175

which he competed were changing, but he was still around the horses and cowboys he loved.

The three toddlers with lives entwined for nearly twenty years were walking on strong and sturdy legs. Each moved in a different direction as the wind carried their dreams to destiny.

Joyce's Memoirs, 1998:

"It was May of nineteen fifty-five. Debra was seventeen months old. Pete was riding barebacks and bulls in Rodeo Cowboys Association-sanctioned rodeos and had entered

Larry Roberts. circa 1955.
(Photos courtesy of Larry Roberts).

a small rodeo in Gilroy. Today they call it the Professional Rodeo Cowboys Association.

"We drove up the night before to meet our friends. That evening, the rodeo secretary told us there was only one entry so far in the Saddle Bronc Riding. She urged Pete and the others to enter the contest and they did.

"When we arrived at the rodeo, Pete checked in and found that he had drawn a horse called, 'Appaloosa,' a big horse with a reputation as a good draw.

"There were now five entries and Pete was the last to ride. All four had qualified, much to the everyone's surprise. That eliminated easy ground money. Pete had to make a good ride to get in the money. He had done well on his bareback horse and was feeling confident when he took hold of the rein on the saddle bronc and gave the nod to open the chute gate.

"Appaloosa came out high and hit the ground hard. He bucked straight and rhythmic. However, at the very last second before the whistle, Appaloosa made a quick move to the left, and Pete went to the right. To my horror, his foot caught in the stirrup. Pete hung like a rag doll off the side of Appaloosa for several jumps.

"Suddenly he came free and fell to the ground. I breathed a huge sigh of relief and in that same instant, Appaloosa gave a powerful kick that connected with Pete's right temple.

"Pete didn't move a muscle as I ran to him in the arena. Fearing he might be dead, I prayed that he wasn't. A couple of cowboys grabbed a stretcher and carried Pete to a room near the rodeo office where a doctor looked him over. While the doctor was putting sutures in the wound, someone called the ambulance. The doctor told me, 'It's not a good sign to see blood coming from the ear; it's an indication of a fractured skull.'

"When the ambulance arrived, they let me ride with him to the hospital where he was transferred to a bed in the hallway and everyone left.

"I kept wondering why nothing was being done. There seemed to be very little staff around. Finally, a nurse came over and just checked to see if he was still alive. I asked her why nothing was being done. She said, 'In these cases, there isn't much to do. If he makes it through the night, he might have a chance to live.'

"The next thing I remember, she was holding something that smelled like ammonia under my nose, and I was lying on the tile floor. According to her, I had been out for several minutes.

"Sometime around five that evening, the doctor that had been on duty at the rodeo arrived. Within minutes, he had everyone jumping. He warned me that Pete's condition was critical, and he might not live. He did say that his chances would improve with every passing hour.

"We had left Debra with my mother to baby-sit. I called and told her what had happened. She made me feel better by telling me not to worry about our daughter. She assured me she would have everyone pray for Pete. I told her what the nurse and doctor had said. She shrugged it off saying, 'What do they know? Pete will be fine. You just trust in God.'

"Pete regained consciousness around five in the morning. As soon as I realized that he recognized me and spoke a couple of words, I knew he would be okay. I said a silent prayer of thanks.

"For the next ten days, I drove back and forth from Salinas to Gilroy. On the morning of his eleventh day in the hospital, they said Pete could go home. Our insurance wouldn't pay for an ambulance to take him thirty miles to Salinas so Marvin and Marguerite put a mattress in the back of their station wagon. Back in our little house on Clay Street, Marvin carried Pete into the house and laid him on the bed. I could never have managed without them.

"Pete was home for about three days when I woke up around midnight with an excruciating pain in my stomach. I crawled to the phone in the kitchen and called my sister, then I woke up in the hospital.

"I was told later that Marvin and Marguerite arrived to find me on the kitchen floor. Pete and Debra were asleep, oblivious to my condition. Marvin carried me to the station wagon cum ambulance and took me to the local hospital while Marguerite stayed with Pete and Debra. Marvin called Doc Weibe who then sent an ambulance for Pete. Doc was outraged that Pete had been sent home [from the other hospital].

"Marvin stayed at the hospital until everything was under control. Doc Weibe found a cyst that had twisted around an ovary. He called Doctor Andresen who took care of me.

"That Sunday in Gilroy ended Pete's career in rough stock riding. He was born with a hearing problem, but the accident made it more severe. It took well over a year for him to get his equilibrium back to normal.

"As I recall this bit of our lives, I realize even more how much Marvin and Marguerite were always there for us."

Joyce was married with a child, Larry had joined the Navy, and Monty left town for college at Cal Poly in San Luis Obispo. The children had grown, reseeding their individual roots, until circumstances would wrap them together again more than forty years later.

Pete and Joyce on their wedding day, March 1, 1953. Also pictured are: Ernie Martins, LaVonne Holt [Kelly], Carol Martins, Pete, Joyce, Jim Martins, Sally Wilson Martins, Harold Kitchel, Joanne Rogers [Crum], Dick Gillott, Tiny Martins Holt, Monty, and Barbara Muller [Fontes].

Part III

An Inkling of Lies

The Red Pony

Billy explained, "Of course we could force-break him to everything, but he wouldn't be as good a horse if we did. He'd always be a little bit afraid, and he wouldn't mind because he wanted to."

—John Steinbeck

Horse and Horseman Training

"I never fight a horse, because they get shook up and can't work. I've got to get their confidence. From there, the rest is easy."

—Marvin E. Roberts

Chapter 10

THE MAN WHO LISTENS?

Monty tirelessly purports his desire to end cycles of violence. He sells a lesson in nonverbal communication to convey messages of kindness and ease fear. It may seem almost mystical. Abused humans find comfort in charismatic words that offer hope.

Those words drip like honey as he paints an eloquent vision of an idyllic world where everyone gets along, violence is gone forever, and relationships can be established in thirty minutes. The concept is brilliantly beautiful. Humans crave it, wanting all to be right with the world as quickly as possible. Monty is embraced by adoring fans around the globe. He convincingly demonstrates the theories and methods he claims, in part, to have discovered while living with wild horses in the Nevada desert.

It's a marvelous concept. In reality, however, it's promoted on a carefully cultivated history of imagined experiences and premises. It's an ingenious scheme.

If this scheme ultimately brings about a societal change for the betterment of humankind and equines, is it wrong? Does anyone care if the reputations of two good and decent people are sacrificed on the altar of greed?

Yes. There are people that care deeply. Those family members and former friends who had their hearts ripped out by Monty's words that cut as surely as Jack the Ripper's knife cut the flesh of his victims. Those family members and former friends who stood by Monty, believed in him, and cheered for him from the sidelines for sixty years were the first to be carved. He cut none so

185

deep as his deceased parents, his confused brother, and his feisty aunt. The question so often asked is, "Why?" Why did he do it?

Is Monty Roberts really making the world a better place for horses as he claims? Is that his true mission? How long have Equus and Join-Up been part of his repertoire? This is, perhaps, the best time to examine the questions, answers, and patterns of a life that appears to have been built on craftiness and greed.

It seems there is a chasm between fiction and nonfiction in literature. Monty Roberts wrote a nonfiction book published by Random House. The book was interesting, but the book was fiction. Those who knew Marvin were upset by Monty's allegations against his father, but in reality, that was only one of the many fabrications plastered across the pages of his book.

Agents, publishers, and those "in the know" said not to write a book to refute another book. The following is a composite of several conversations that this book's authors had with editors, publishers, and attorneys. It is included here as a single conversation only to provide a sense of understanding.

"You cannot write a book to refute an already published book."

"Why not?"

"Because it's not done."

"Why not?"

"Because. That sounds more like a magazine article or an exposé."

"It's more complicated than that."

"Then what's the pitch? Why would anyone want to read it? What's the story?"

"It's complicated. It's a story of two people who dedicated their lives to horses and humans."

"That's not good enough. Nobody will publish that. You're wasting your time."

"It's a story about life. It's a story about love of humanity. It's a story about greed. Most of all, it's a story about relationships."

"Relationships?"

"Yes, relationships."

"Between?"

"Between humans and between humans and horses."

"Isn't that what Monty is trying to sell?"

"Yes, but he is selling the *Cliff Notes* version of relationships. He is selling a relationship that takes thirty minutes to establish. Many people believe that relationship is supposed to last a lifetime."

"Does his system work?"

"It appears to. But there are men who can charm a woman right out of her panties. It doesn't mean they have established a meaningful relationship. In time, she'll wise up. That's when the explosion hits."

"Do you think that same thing will happen with horses? Is that your book's premise?"

"We don't know what the long-term effects are on a horse from a thirty-minute love affair with Monty Roberts. He says there are ten thousand or more horses he started this way."

"The guy gets around."

"The point is not whether or not the relationship can be established with the horse. The point is the importance of meaning in our lives. Where does it come from? Do we derive our reason for being from the accolades received through shallow, thirty-minute relationships and the dollar amount of our bank accounts? Or should we be defined by who we are when all the layers are peeled away and we are willing to bare our most inner selves to those with whom we have established a meaningful relationship?"

"Is this a psychology book? You have no credentials for that. Are you talking about marriage? I'm a bit confused."

"It's a book about people—ordinary people and extraordinary people. It's about relationships—all relationships, not just those between men and women. Humans can and do establish core connections and deep emotional relationships with horses. They bond."

"Are you telling me that Monty bonds with a horse in thirty minutes?"

"So it appears. We don't challenge that. We challenge his life history and that of his family. We challenge his true, deep, core, when-no-one-is-looking methods of getting to the top. We challenge his right to publicly, and knowingly, make false, unsubstantiated statements that ruined the valued reputations and good names of his deceased parents."

"Aren't there courts for that?"

"It's reputed that his book has sold more than two million copies around the world. Who is going to tell all those people the truth? Don't they have a right to know? Isn't the publishing industry under some obligation to insure that nonfiction literature is *somewhat* close to the truth?"

"Yes. Most publishers require a signed statement of truth from the author when printing nonfiction. That doesn't mean the author can't lie. People lie all the time."

"Instead of taking him to court, which only a handful of people will ever hear about, three generations of humans who were shocked and outraged by Monty's lies about his parents united to write a book that tells the real truth about his life and that of his family."

"It'll never sell. You're wasting your time."

"Maybe we are. Maybe the entire family and all of Monty's old friends are wasting their time too, but this is something we have to do. We have to do this for Marvin and Marguerite and for everyone who believes that readers of nonfiction deserve the truth."

"Good luck to you. You're going to need it. Have you thought that he might file a lawsuit against you?"

"Yes, we thought of that. We also thought we should be the ones filing the lawsuit against him. He can and will do whatever he wants. Everything written in this book has been thoroughly documented. There are hundreds of people willing to testify, under oath, as to the validity of the statements made here."

"Aren't Monty's exploits also supposed to be well documented?"

"So he makes people believe, but he cannot document things that never happened."

An Inkling of Lies

Interview with LaVonne Holt Kelley, Marguerite's niece and student, 1998:

"The first inkling I had that Monty was telling lies was in a book by Jack Canfield and Mark Victor Hansen called Chicken Soup for the Soul.[17] *Everyone told me it was great and it had inspiring stories about people who had reached their goals despite great adversity. I found*

---

[17] Jack Canfield and Mark Victor Hansen, *Chicken Soup for the Soul,* (Deerfield Beach, FL, Health Communications, Inc., 1993).

Monty's so-called [true] story in the book. The idea that it was printed as true made me doubt the validity of [Chicken Soup for the Soul].

"Monty is obviously so egocentric that it is ridiculous. He would do anything for attention. Apparently, he would malign his deceased parents to further his own financial gain and notoriety."

ACCUSATIONS OF DREAM STEALING

In the first edition of *Chicken Soup for the Soul* (1993) by Jack Canfield and Mark Victor Hansen, a short story is told about Monty Roberts.

Canfield wrote that his friend, Monty Roberts, owns a horse ranch and beautiful home in San Ysidro that he lets Canfield use as a venue for fund-raising events.

According to Canfield, Monty told the assembled group, "I want to tell you why I let Jack use my house. It all goes back to a story about a young man who was the son of an itinerant horse trainer who would go from stable to stable, race track to race track, farm to farm, and ranch to ranch, training horses. As a result, the boy's high school career was continually interrupted.[18] When he was a senior, the boy was asked to write a paper about what he wanted to be and do when he grew up.

"That night he wrote a seven-page paper describing his goal of someday owning a horse ranch. He wrote about his dream in great detail and he even drew a diagram of a two-hundred-acre ranch, showing the location of all the buildings, the stables, and the track. Then he

---

[18] Monty and his parents actually lived in only *one* house throughout his four years of high school.

drew a detailed floor plan for a four-thousand-square-foot house that would sit on the two-hundred-acre dream ranch.

"He put a great deal of his heart into the project, and the next day he handed it in to his teacher. Two days later he received his paper back. On the front page was a large red F with a note that read, 'See me after class.'

"The boy with the dream went to see the teacher after class and asked, 'Why did I receive an F?'

"The teacher said, 'This is an unrealistic dream for a young boy like you. You have no money. You come from an itinerant family. You have no resources. Owning a horse ranch requires a lot of money. You have to buy the land. You have to pay for the original breeding stock, and later you'll have to pay large stud fees. There's no way you could ever do it.' Then the teacher added, 'If you will rewrite this paper with a more realistic goal, I will reconsider your grade.'

"The boy went home and thought about it long and hard. He asked his father[19] what he should do. His father said, 'Look, son, you have to make up your own mind on this. However, I think it is a very important decision for you.'

"Finally, after sitting with it for a week, the boy turned in the same paper, making no changes at all. He stated, 'You can keep the F, and I'll keep my dream.' "

Monty then added, "I tell you this story because you are sitting in my four-thousand-square-foot house in the middle of my two-hundred-acre horse ranch. I still have that school paper framed over the fireplace." He added,

[19] In *The Man Who Listens to Horses,* Monty writes that he went to his *mother* for advice.

"The best part of the story is that two summers ago that same schoolteacher brought thirty kids to camp out on my ranch for a week." When the teacher was leaving, he said, 'Look, Monty, I can tell you this now. When I was your teacher, I was something of a dream stealer. During those years I stole a lot of kids' dreams. Fortunately, you had enough gumption not to give up on yours.' "

Like most of the stories in *Chicken Soup for the Soul*, it's an uplifting story with a message of courage and hope.

From the fantastic popularity of books like *Chicken Soup for the Soul* and television programs like *Touched by an Angel*, the genuine need for stories that feed the human spirit is realized. Talk show hostess Oprah Winfrey also found this niche. Her programming often fills a very real, very human need for goodness.

The messengers that touch the human spirit are to be commended and applauded. By offering courage, hope, and spiritual strength to others, they espouse goodness. That's the reason many people said the truth about Monty Roberts should not be told.

His supporters call him a messenger of goodness to humans and horses. He raises money for charity. His supporters say he has done no harm. Doesn't the truth matter anymore?

In *The Man Who Listens to Horses*, Monty made four perceptible changes to the story found in *Chicken Soup for the Soul*. In *The Man Who Listens to Horses:* he omitted being the son of an itinerant; he says he went to his mother, rather than to his father for advice; and he said the teacher brought geriatrics to the farm instead of students. He also gave the teacher a name: Mr. Lyman Fowler.

Lyman Fowler taught agricultural science at Hartnell Junior College in the early 1950s. At that time, his classes were also open to high school juniors and seniors. Fowler was a favorite among students and most remember him fondly. Yet Monty contends in both stories that Mr. Fowler admitted that he tried to cap the aspirations of his students.

Lyman Fowler was shocked when he learned about Monty's odious accusation against him and by Monty's preposterous comment that Mr. Fowler had admitted to the moral crime. In 1998, the distinguished octogenarian said that throughout his years of teaching, he could not recall giving an assignment like the one Monty described. Mr. Fowler did, however, believe it was possible that he had given Monty a failing grade on a project, but didn't remember doing so.

In the early 1990s or late 1980s, Mr. Fowler rode a tour bus that stopped to visit Monty's farm in Solvang, California. Though he was not the guide, as Monty infers, Fowler did see and speak with Monty on that day. However, Fowler said, the conversation was nothing like Monty described.

Interview with Kent Fowler, Salinas veterinarian, 1998:

"Monty's description of [Lyman] as a dream stealer is entirely out of [Lyman's] character. That is not the kind of thing [my father] would do, and that is not the kind of person he is.

"I didn't have the stomach to read all of Monty's book. I forced myself to read the two sections that involved my dad, who is eighty-six. [What I read] made me sick."

Another innocent victim—pierced by another lie. This was no little lie. This lie was well designed to stir emotional embers. This whisper was not so quiet.

Mother was Meek?

It is difficult for anyone who knew Marguerite Roberts to believe she could ever be described as meek or subservient. Everyone saw her as the disciplinarian in the family.

Interview with Lou Martins, Marguerite's brother, 1997:

"My big sister never knew the meaning of the words meek, mousy, or subservient. She was a stern disciplinarian and a rule maker. She was outspoken and loud and she was tough as leather. Anyone who knew her will tell you this. But Marguerite was always one to help too.

"She stood up for what was right and blasted anyone she felt had done wrong. It didn't matter who they were."

1957, San Diego, California

It was after one of the last games of Navy's football season that it happened. Players and guests had gathered for an awards banquet.

People were milling around, jockeying for seats in the crowded room. A woman near Marguerite was having trouble with a folding chair when one of the players moved to assist her. The eighteen-year-old halfback with a boyish smile and freckles across his nose tugged at the chair wedged under the table.

Too late, Marguerite noticed the chair leg. The gray metal had weakened near the seat. The angle was wrong. It wasn't going to hold. The woman was on her way down.

The warning died on Marguerite's lips. The young man's smile wilted as the woman, chair, and tray of food crashed to the highly polished linoleum floor.

The clattering sound of USN-issue metal utensils and plates filled the air. The cacophony of voices in the room fell silent as people turned to stare. Marguerite set her own tray on the nearest table and was moving to assist the mortified woman when someone called, "Attention on Deck!" and all military personnel jumped up—starched stiff and dead-man still. An apparently high ranking naval commander had entered the room at the precise moment the woman's ample bottom hit the deck.

The ball player stood next to the woman on the floor. He had grabbed the chair in a failed attempt to stop her fall and was now standing at attention, chair in hand, not sure what to do next.

After a quick survey of the situation, the officer began to berate the seaman for incompetence. The accusations he leveled were more than Marguerite could tolerate as she watched the young man take the verbal abuse.

Marguerite had witnessed the fall. The sailor was not at fault. *Oh no you don't,* she thought.

All eyes and ears were on the officer. No one dared to speak. Not even the woman on the floor would refute the officer's misconception.

I've heard enough, Marguerite thought as she stepped with determination toward the officer who had steel gray eyes and a personality to match. Their eyes met. His voice dropped an octave. He paused, ostensibly to put the men at ease and release the tension his presence and diatribe had created. Marguerite seized the moment of opportunity.

"Well now, I've seen it all," she bellowed, pulling her voice up from the diaphragm like she did when issuing commands to students in the arena. All eyes shifted to Marguerite.

Larry wished that he could crawl under a table. Marvin smiled and waited to see what dish his darling wife was about to serve the officer. The only person moving in the room was Marguerite. She was loud enough to be heard in the kitchen.

"Just *who* do you think you are?" she asked.

Shocked to be addressed in such a manner, the commander stared as she made her approach.

"I beg your pardon, ma'am?" he managed. His strong voice now carried an edge of doubt.

"You come in here, take one look at an *accident,* and start blaming that young man," she said, close enough now that he could smell the Enigma perfume she wore. He stepped back. She moved forward. All eyes were riveted on the scene.

"He was just trying to help," said Marguerite, pointing to the football player who stared in amazement.

"We all saw it," her sweeping arm encompassed the room.

"You don't get any of the facts. You don't ask what happened. You just ridiculed. And for your information, that young man didn't do anything wrong."

Larry watched in awe and dread as his mother got in the face of this superior officer. She was inching forward with each word, and the officer was shuffling back toward the door. He wanted nothing to do with the woman who looked meaner than a Gunny Marine denied liberty.

"You owe him an apology." She waggled her forefinger. "But maybe you should just leave. We were having a real good time before you showed up."

They had reached the door before he took his eyes off her to look about the room. He had no allies in the crowd. Without a word, he turned and left.

When Marguerite spun from the door, still shaking with anger, she was met with a standing ovation from the crowd.

Larry-the-son was mortified. Larry-the-football-playing-military-man was button-popping proud of his take-names and kick-butt mother. He may have wanted to crawl under a table, but he also wanted to hug and kiss her at the same time. The football team rewarded Marguerite with an autographed football and made her their honorary mascot.

Monty says his mother was meek and subservient? Those words cannot be used to describe the woman everyone else knew as Marguerite 'Flick' Roberts.

CAL POLY

Monty sells himself as a man committed to making this a better world for horses and humans. Though his Join-Up methodology is not new, nor even unique, people flock to see this charismatic and eloquent man. It appears to be a classic example of the old confidence game—on a grand scale.

Monty asks us to believe that he wants to make a better world for horses. He tells us this has been his desire since he was a young boy. He tells us that he couldn't wait to get away from his father so that he could use these humane training methods.

The Man Who Listens to Horses:
> Behind my father's back [around 1953 or earlier]
> I had started to investigate the silent language of
> Equus. I could not wait to be free of him and to
> start using my own methods. (p.94)

1955–1957, SAN LUIS OBISPO, CALIFORNIA

Among the cowboy students at California's Polytechnic State College, the name Monty Roberts was synonymous with *winner*. He competed at many of the local horse shows with other students who were honing skills and seeking to improve their horsemanship.

Forty years later, Monty's former college pals were easy to find. They remember Monty well. Oddly, they also remember his father. None of them wanted their names mentioned in a book.

None wanted to test the wrath of Monty Roberts. None were willing to chance the mettle of his venom.

Monty, like his teammates, kept horses at school. When it came time to enter a horse show, however, Monty called his dad. With a list of classes his son wanted to enter, Marvin loaded a trailer in Salinas with his own best horses, specialists in each event. From there, he made the two-and-a-half hour drive to meet Monty, who showed the champions as his own.

As one former classmate put it, "We didn't have a snowball's chance in hell against him. The rest of us were pretty jealous. Monty's parents would drive almost one hundred twenty-five miles, one-way, to help him win and to watch him compete. Nobody else's parents ever did anything like that. And it wasn't just a one-time deal either. Marvin was down at Cal Poly all the time when we were going to school there."

198

"I'd say that's pretty nice. Wouldn't you?" he queried.

That classmate went on to make a name for himself in the performance horse world. Before his death in 1998, he told Monty's relatives and several other people that he was ashamed of what Monty had done. "I feel bad for the family because it's not right. But it's his thing and his business. It's not my place to say anything publicly.

Cal Poly Rodeo Team Visited Salinas

The photo caption in a 1957 edition of the Salinas Californian *reads: "CAL POLY RODEO TEAM recently stopped off in Salinas to visit with Mr. and Mrs. Marvin Roberts at the California Rodeo grounds. . . . Mr. Roberts, at right, above, points out some of the features of the local rodeo grounds to team members. Standing from the left are Greg Ward of Bakersfield and Bill Stroud of San Jose, team captain; on chutes, George "Hoot" Putnam of Santa Maria, Scott Reddington of Sheridan, Wyo., Marvin Roberts, Jr., Salinas; Larry Fanning of Martin, So. Dakota, and Bill Nielson of Santa Cruz. . . . Marvin, Jr., took first place in cutting horse class and pleasure horse class at Cal Poly's recent Poly Royal and also placed fourth in stock horse class."*

I'm gonna see him and I'm gonna say somethin' to him—
to his face. His parents were real good to us when we
used to go through Salinas."

As the Cal Poly rodeo team traveled the western
states on the intercollegiate circuit, they often passed
through Salinas. Invariably, Monty and members of the
team stopped to visit Marvin and Marguerite Roberts
at the rodeo grounds. Always hospitable and kind, the
students knew they could count on Monty's parents to
help them with food or lodging.

The memories of Monty's college pals paint a different picture of the student who claimed he wanted to be
free of his father so that he could use his own methods
to train horses. They paint a different picture of the man
who later said he had longed for the moment when he
could stand over his dead father.

1955–1959, Rodeo Grounds, Salinas

Activity at the rodeo grounds didn't slow because
Monty, Larry, and Joyce were gone. A new generation of
students and proteges were winning awards and riding
in the old blue van.

Interview with Leah Rogers Gross, Roberts student, 1998:

*"I was in kindergarten at Lincoln School when
Marguerite first started to pick me up with the
older children for riding lessons. Marvin was still
a policeman then. I remember how he used to
tease me by putting handcuffs on me. He always
looked surprised when I laughed and slipped
them off my little hands.*

*"When I was growing up, my parents traveled
a lot, so much of my time was spent with Marvin*

200

and Marguerite. They were like my second set of parents. Back in those days, I think they probably knew me better than my own parents knew me.

"I got my own horse when I was six: a big black mare named Bambi. Through the next ten years, and five horses, nearly all of my waking, nonschool hours were spent at the rodeo grounds. It was my second home and the Roberts were my second family until we moved to San Jose in nineteen fifty-nine.

"Marvin and Marguerite had their rules: the do's and don'ts around the barn. Sometimes we got in trouble [for breaking the rules], but I never remember either of them coming unglued over something we did that was wrong. There was certainly never any physical punishment.

"Marguerite always said I was like a daughter to her. In fact, my thirteenth birthday party was held in their backyard in the mid–nineteen fifties. Marvin barbecued for all the guests. My own parents were out of town.

"Most important to me were the horse shows we attended nearly every weekend, spring through fall. Many of the shows were nearby, but I thought the highlight was always the Junior Grand National at the Cow Palace in San Francisco.

"Marvin pulled an old house trailer behind the big blue horse van. The trailer was our traveling tack and dressing room. It was always a great adventure to go the Grand National

[Horse Show] and stay in a motel with the other riders.

"They helped us get ready for our classes and always made sure we looked our best. They also made sure we ate healthy meals and not a lot of junk food.

"How the Roberts kept track of us is beyond my comprehension. We could be a rowdy group of kids, but they generally kept a tight rein on us. I think most of us were a pain, but Marvin and Marguerite were always there for us, no matter what."

Interview with Marion Johnson Scheffler, Roberts student, 1998:

"The Roberts were extremely important to me in my preteen years.

"My dream as a child and teenager growing up in Salinas was to ride horses and become the California Rodeo Hostess. Many little girls had this dream, but Marvin and Marguerite Roberts made this dream come true for me.

"As I entered Washington Junior High School, my parents decided to help me work toward my dream. Where did we start? The answer was, of course, with Marvin and Marguerite Roberts. We boarded our horses with the Roberts, and every day I would go to the stables to exercise and ride my horses.

"This loving, compassionate couple taught me to ride. They worked with my parents to find good horses for me to enjoy, and they helped me work

to fulfill that everlasting wish to become the Hostess.

"In nineteen fifty-six, my dream came true. I became California Rodeo Hostess. The contest judged a young woman on scholarship, personality, appearance, and horsemanship. Horsemanship counted the most, and at that point in time, I really knew how to ride, thanks to Marvin and Marguerite Roberts.

"Let us go back a little farther in time and address the accusations of Monty Roberts in his book, magazine articles, newspaper articles, and talk shows. Monty paints a picture of his mother as a meek woman and of his father as a cruel violent man who not only beat his horses, but beat Monty also. I simply never did see this.

"For eight years [1948–1956], I spent every day after school, weekends, and summers at the stables. In all those years, I never witnessed Marvin Roberts being cruel to his sons or his horses. What I did witness was the expert horsemanship displayed by both Larry and Monty Roberts.

"To watch them ride was to see poetry in motion. Where do you suppose they learned this? Of course, they learned it from their loving parents Marvin and Marguerite.

"The Roberts devoted their lives to young people who rode horses. I have fond memories of riding with the junior horsemen to the top of Fremont's Peak for a weekend adventure. We rode *as a group in parades. All the kids loved Marvin and Marguerite. They always had time for us.*

"I am proud to be able to say that Marvin and Marguerite Roberts were two wonderful, loving people. I adored them for having a positive effect on my life, and I thank them for making my dream become a reality."

Interview with Kathryn Riley, Mother of student, 1997:

"I have great love and respect for Marguerite and Marvin Roberts and have always said they did more for the children of Monterey County [than most anyone else], and I've lived and worked here since nineteen forty-one.

"In nineteen fifty-five, we boarded our horses at the rodeo grounds so my daughter, Brenda, could take lessons and compete in the horse shows. For five years we had personal contact with the Roberts each day and never saw Marvin violent with anyone or with a horse.

"They made learning fun for the students and never lost patience with a child or a horse. Like parents to all, they shared their love with each of them. Marvin and Marguerite were a wonderful couple and the only people whom I trusted to take my daughter to a show on those few occasions that her father or I couldn't go."

Interview with Andrée Forzani, horse trainer, 1998:

"I was proud to know both Marguerite and Marvin. I took lessons from Marvin and saw them often at horse shows. They were both expert

and hard working at their craft. They ran their training facility at the Salinas Rodeo Grounds with integrity and fairness, plus a lot of hard work.

"In the late nineteen fifties, I was riding in the San Juan Bautista horse parade with my husband, Roy. Marvin was there too. I was on a young quarter horse gelding in the hackamore. The parade was just ending, and we were waiting for the horse show and rodeo to begin. This was my first real hackamore horse, and I didn't have the presence of mind to drop my reins and give the colt's nose and neck a rest.

"He was a soft little horse and wasn't going to go anywhere. I think I was mentally elsewhere, gawking at the crowds.

"Marvin noticed my horse's predicament. I remember him saying softly, 'You can let him down now.' This was a gentle reminder to think of my horse first. I thank Marvin to this day for that comment. He helped me realize that this simple act of mind and hand at the correct time is one of the cornerstones of horsemanship."

Growing Families

Within a very short span of years, several additions were made to the families.

By 1956, Joyce and Pete Renebome had their second child. A boy this time, Jeff joined his two-and-a-half-year-old sister, Debra. Cheri was born in 1957.

In June 1956, Monty married Pat Burden and their first child, Deborah, was born less than a year later. Pat gave birth to two more children, Laurel and Marty, within a few more years. Monty and Pat continued to live and work near San Luis Obispo.

Meanwhile, Larry married his sweetheart, Patsy, who had a baby girl in 1957. They named her Lynn.

THE MARTINS FAMILY

While Joyce, Monty, and Larry were starting their families, an era was ending for the Martins family.

Since 1924, Papa Martins had been a fisherman. Usually gone for months at a time, Frank cast his nets from Catalina to Santa Cruz until his death in 1958. He was sixty-seven when God called him home early on Christmas morning. All eight of his children had been there on Christmas Eve. He had played with his grandchildren and told them tales of the sea as they watched the cigar smoke curl around his head in wide-eyed wonder.

When Papa went to bed that night, Mame was still up, putting things away in the kitchen. He knocked on the headboard one last time, his signal for her to join him in the double bed they shared.

Mame continued to live in the house at 601 El Camino Real North until she died in 1966. She was picking green beans in the garden when she suffered a massive heart attack. Perhaps she heard Frank knocking on the headboard one last time, calling her to join him.

Chapter 11

More of Marvin's Methods

Marvin Roberts method of training a horse dated back to the early California Spanish vaqueros. A horse trained in this method could be ridden with the slightest touch of the rider's little finger. These horses were referred to as *light mouthed*. Ridden properly, they stayed light mouthed for the rest of their life. Marvin used to say that a properly trained horse could easily be ridden without a bridle or using only twine string for reins. There was no need to pull a horse with a heavy hand.

The great horsemanship practiced by the early vaqueros was based on the training methods of the Spanish Light Cavalry. Two of the most necessary attributes needed were patience and finesse. Marvin possessed an abundance of both.

Different reining equipment was used at various stages of training: the hackamore, the double-rein, and the bridle. Marvin started his horses using a hackamore.

The Spanish called it *jaquima*. The hackamore consists of a sturdy *bosal*—braided rawhide shaped into a noseband and held in place by a thin strip of leather over the horse's head and behind his ears—and a *mecáte*—a horse hair rope attached to the bottom of the noseband and fashioned into reins.

The hackamore, used properly, was not cruel or severe. Marvin cautioned readers of the training manual he published in 1957, called *Horse and Horseman Training,* never to pull too hard on the hackamore. He also advised his readers to wrap the noseband of the hackamore with a thick sheepskin fleece to protect the horse's tender nose.

Interview with Betty Dolan Kent, family friend, 1997:

"For some time, Marvin had been writing a book on the breaking and training of horses. He was doing it in longhand, and I remember it was an arduous process. I offered to take dictation in shorthand and type it up so he could recheck it. We did this a couple of nights a week while Marguerite cleaned up after dinner and the boys did their homework. After Marvin finished a rough draft, I retyped it, and he took the manuscript to someone that could turn it into a real book.[20]"

In the very early stages of training with a hackamore, the horse's chin can become tender (more on this later). Horses are highly skin-sensitive, but the sensation can best be described as similar to that of a child with a scraped knee on the playground; it is tender, but a kiss, a Band-Aid, and a reminder of the warning not to run will work wonders to cure the hurt. The child soon forgets the minor stinging sensation but remembers not to run when told to walk.

Whenever a horse did suffer a scraped chin, however, Marvin covered the sore with his special medical

---

[20] *Horse and Horseman Training* is a sixty-page hardcover book. It was self-published in 1957 by Marvin and lithographed by the El Camino Press in Salinas. The dust jacket carries a photograph of Larry on Oriole and Monty on Brownie.

concoction made of a sulfur-based salve. The soreness never lasted more than a few days, and the lesson was learned without injury or trauma to the horse.

Like the vaqueros before him, Marvin started horses in the hackamore instead of using a bridle with any type of bit designed to go in the mouth of the horse. He did this to avoid possible damage to the delicate mouth of the horse. A bit placed in the mouth of a horse rests gently on his gums in the open space between front and back teeth. If these bars develop calluses during the initial training process, or at any time, a horse would become known as *hard-mouthed.*

Hackamore

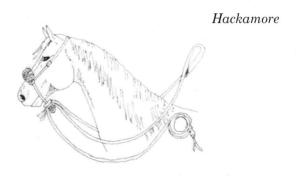

Marvin Roberts was cruel? Is it cruel to let a child use a playground where he might scrape a knee and learn to heed a parent's message?

Once a horse understood the message relayed through Marvin's gentle hands on the hackamore and the two established a mutual trust, Marvin advanced the animal to the double-rein.

The hackamore's sturdy bosal was replaced with one that was pencil thin and extremely lightweight. Along with this new, lightweight hackamore, the horse was introduced to the bridle. Now a bit was placed in the horse's mouth, and he could acclimate gently.

At the start of the double-rein training process, Marvin liked to use a simple mouthpiece known as a *half-breed* bit. Marvin was a master with the double-rein. His feather-light touch on the reins cued the horse with delicate signals. Through the double-rein combination, the horse learned to feel the delicate difference and understand Marvin's minute cues through the bit in his mouth. As Marvin gradually took the horse through the change of headgear, he was careful to also keep his body signals consistent. That helped the horse understand the message being relayed.

Double-Rein

With consistent training over time, the horse remembered the combination of signals from Marvin and transferred them to the new signals he felt through the bit in his mouth. He understood what was being asked, because it had been asked before, and he gladly obliged.

Marvin thus prepared the horse to trust him, his signals, and his guidance. Through Marvin's gentle hands on the reins and the many nuances of his body language, Marvin and his horse became a team. Reliant on each other, Marvin and the horse found joy in their relationship. Without force, without dominance, without abuse, and without fear, they worked as a single unit.

Eventually, the double-rein was removed and the horse would graduate to become a *bridle horse.* He would then be known as *straight-up* in the bridle. As the horse became thoroughly accustomed to the bridle, Marvin often advanced him to a mouthpiece known as the *spade-bit.* He also liked one called the *Salinas.* The whole process often took several years to complete. It was not forced and was not undertaken in thirty minutes or thirty days.

Anyone familiar with the old Spanish vaquero training process could draw a mount from a large remuda and know the level of training the horse had received with but a glance at his withers. An untrimmed mane meant an unridden horse. One with a mane clipped smooth over the withers was ridden in the hackamore. A horse with a mane clipped over the withers, but with two small tufts, one-inch apart and one-inch long, was ridden in the double-rein. A mount that bore a single one-inch tuft of mane above his withers was a bridle horse, a veteran.

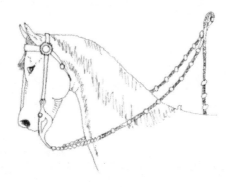

In the Bridle

None of the equipment used in Marvin's seasoned, gentle hands was ever cruel or severe. The horse was always his first consideration. Marvin often waited until a horse was three or four years old before he began training, giving the horse time to mature as an individual. Today, large money purses offered in futurities and society's harried pace, tempts owners and trainers to push a horse and rush his training before his legs and bones are completely developed. All too often the tragedy of permanent physical damage is a result of human impatience.

Another controversial area of training that has come under fire as cruel is the process called *sacking-out*. Marvin strongly believed all young horses should learn early that there was nothing to fear from humans. A horse that felt fear could easily hurt himself and the humans around him, not by intent, but by his sheer size and flight reaction to the unknown.

Marvin's method of sacking-out began by restraining the horse with a soft cotton rope. Just as a father might hold his toddler while introducing him to a fearful-looking dog that is actually a friendly family pet, Marvin held the horse and introduced him to a piece of cloth or plastic tied to a rope—the sack.

He first tossed the sack on the ground near the horse, dragging it away by holding and pulling on the attached rope. All the while Marvin spoke softly to reassure the horse. As the animal became accustomed to the sack, Marvin tossed it lightly against his legs. He continued to talk to the horse and gently toss and retrieve the sack. The sack would eventually be tossed onto, and pulled off of, the rump, back, neck, and head of the horse, while he stood docilely, accustomed to the perhaps annoying, but nonthreatening, nonfrightening, object.

After a short time, the horse would not be bothered when the sack was tossed. Through Marvin's soothing words and the light touch of the sack, he learned there was nothing to fear. It was Marvin's professional opinion that a horse that had never been sacked out could have a serious flaw in his training. He had seen too many riders and horses hurt because an otherwise well-trained horse shied or bolted from a wind-blown piece of paper, a hat, or a flag carried in a parade.

A CNN newscast on December 1, 1998, captured a surprise mishap involving a horse. It seems one of the Queen's horses in a public parade shied and reared, dumping the red-coated rider with an unceremonious pomp to the pavement. A horse that has not learned to accept surprises can be dangerous. It is reputed that the Queen's horses are now started using Monty's thirty-minute process.

There is a right way and a wrong way to conduct any training program. Monty Roberts publicly accuses his father Marvin of using cruel and abusive methods to break and train horses. In a video produced about Monty and aired on the Public Broadcasting System, there is a scene that shows the harsh handling of a horse that is supposedly in training. During this scene, the narrator talks about Marvin's cruel program. The inference, it appears, is that the abusive handler is Marvin. It is most definitely not Marvin and the method shown is not the way Marvin conducted his training program. Sadly, a horse somewhere may have been forced to suffer some possible emotional trauma while that segment was filmed for Monty.

Readers of Monty's book were appalled to see a photo of Marvin with a horse bound in ropes and lying on its side. They were convinced that Marvin tied his horses up to gain supremacy.

The photograph was actually taken to explain the method and show the procedure of laying a horse down if you intended to neuter a stallion or to doctor a wound. In the 1950s, most experienced horse handlers possessed a lot of veterinary knowledge. Marvin was no exception. A veterinarian might not be immediately available and knowing how to lay a horse down to administer emergency medical treatment might mean the difference between life and death for a horse with a severe injury.

1998, A NOTE ABOUT *THE HORSE WHISPERER*

Monty has publicly decried a particular scene in the movie *The Horse Whisperer*, directed by and starring Robert Redford. In the scene, a horse is required to lie down. Throughout the filming, representatives from the American Humane Association (AHA) were on hand to protect the horses from any possible abuse. The AHA ensures animals receive a standard of care that far exceeds the mere prevention of cruelty.

The director of AHA's Film and TV Unit, Gini Barrett, personally supervised the scene Monty has most criticized. What follows is an excerpt from a four-page news release written by Gini Barrett and issued by the AHA and titled, "American Humane Association Condemns False Statements by Monty Roberts":

> [I] personally supervised the scene Monty Roberts has most criticized—when Pilgrim is gently brought to a lying down position utilizing a rope around a front hoof to shift the horse's center of gravity. In the actual filming of the scene, [two

horses] were used to play Pilgrim. Both are well-trained horses, and were completely relaxed throughout the film sequence. Lying down is a familiar and simple request for them, and the rope merely an aspect of their wardrobe. At no time during the filming of this sequence was any animal stressed or placed at risk.

While Monty Roberts does not approve of this technique, and that is certainly his right, other compassionate and excellent natural horsemanship trainers can and do use it humanely. Could this technique be used in an abusive manner? Certainly—as could almost any practice. Monty Roberts has stated in several interviews that his father used a similar technique in a cruel manner. Perhaps he needs to watch other trainers work and learn how it might be done properly.

Marvin's horses were a joy to work with and to show. Often called *bomb proof*, most could be ridden with a thin piece of twine for reins. Marvin did not use *any* training technique in *any* sort of cruel manner, though millions of people now believe that he did. Perhaps Monty does need to watch other trainers work and remember how his father really trained horses.

Interview with Alan Balch, friend and student, 1997:

"I arrived in Salinas in nineteen fifty-seven to fulfill a teaching contract. It was in the fall of nineteen sixty when I first met Marvin and Marguerite Roberts. With future aspirations of owning a horse, I wanted riding lessons. After making inquiries, I was told that the Roberts were the people I should contact.

"We met in the arena of the California Rodeo

215

Grounds, now the Salinas Sports Complex. They were just finishing with a class of young riders. I instantly took a liking to them, and it was the beginning of a twenty-five-year friendship.

"Youngsters and teens were always in attendance at the Roberts facility. I was soon enrolled in riding classes with many of the young riders, who, to my eyes, seemed accomplished horsemen and women. Indeed, many went on to become competitors and trainers in the horse world. Eventually, under the proven instruction of the Roberts, I became a passable horseman too.

"Both took part in the training sessions, and they weren't reticent in sharing their instructions. Where Marvin might discreetly point out my deficiencies, Marguerite would shout from her position in the center of the riding ring: 'Alan! What are you doing? Control that horse and collect yourself! Sit up straight and get those heels down.' I'm sure that in that group of young people, I must have stood out as the class dunce. Through sheer perseverance, I survived.

"I have many fond memories of the swell times we had with the students and owners who boarded their horses with the Roberts. There were play days, beach and trail rides, horse shows, rodeos, and gymkhanas. And always, always, food, barbecues, picnics, and potlucks. Marguerite always had room at her table and food for an extra person.

"I had met their sons, Monty and Larry, after

they were grown men, so I can't say that I knew them well; however, their parents talked about them both frequently. It was obvious they were proud of their sons' horsemanship and accomplishments.

"They were also proud of their students, both past and present. As I mentioned earlier, there were always kids around and during weekends, holidays, and summers. Many of them were present all day.

"I often thought of the Roberts as being surrogate parents to these young people. They gave them their attention, love, and discipline. Although they were allowed to have fun, the Roberts didn't brook any nonsense or tolerate any sass. Years later they stayed in contact with former students and valued highly that association.

"The Monterey County Junior Horsemen's Association was a priority and love of theirs long before I arrived on the scene.

"Marvin was president of the Sheriff's posse three times. He was an active member who took particular interest in the Junior Rodeo and a parade rider. Everyone on the parade route knew or recognized Marvin and Marguerite as they rode by. Before his death, the arena at the posse grounds was renamed the Marvin E. Roberts Arena in his honor. It was fitting since he had contributed so much to the organization since its founding.

"Marvin and Marguerite were not super-

human. They were normal citizens like most of us with faults like any of us. They lived a good life, loved and were loved, and affected the lives of countless individuals."

Interview with Pam Hoffmann King, Roberts student, 1997:

"I started riding lessons at the rodeo grounds in Salinas in the late nineteen fifties. As many before me, I rode Boots. I had two private lessons before going into the class lessons. At first, Marvin sat behind me and helped me at the trot and gallop in the arena by the stalls. That first hour flew by, and I could not wait for Marguerite to pick me up the next week in her big station wagon for another lesson. I rode school horses until April of nineteen sixty when Marvin helped my dad find my first horse, Jumbolia.

"I have owned a horse or horses ever since that day. My husband and I just got a bigger place so we have more room for our horses.

"The junior horsemen's association was an important part of my life back then. One meeting I will always remember was the evening we got to go to the barn and see Jane Muzinich's mare and foal. It was my first time seeing a newborn foal.

"Marvin had them in the first stall, full of fresh straw. We talked about the foal, and I was full of questions. Marvin helped me understand everything. I must have been nine or ten.

"I rode with Marvin through high school. I bought one of the best horses I have ever owned

from him. Her name was Deborah Lynn, named after two of his granddaughters. I went on to win many local and state competitions on Debbie.

"From junior horsemen meetings, riding lessons, showing horses, beach rides, overnight rides, riding in the California Rodeo Parade, I have nothing but fond and fun memories of my youth. Marvin and Marguerite were a huge part of my childhood that I will always treasure. My stories are endless.

"If there ever were a time when Marvin could have lost his temper, which he did not, it would have been at the King City Fair.

"Jane Muzinich and I were told to get our horses ready for the show. We did have the horses saddled, but we were not at all ready. Thinking we had lots of time before our classes, we walked over to the carnival. We were riding The Hammer when they called Jane's class on the loudspeaker. We got off the ride and ran. We ran as fast as we could. We just knew that Marvin was going to kill us; it was an expression used at the time. He had never even lost his temper with us. That didn't matter. We knew what he expected, and we had not met those expectations.

"When we got to the trailer, Marvin was there. He helped Jane get into her chaps, bridled her horse, and told her to go and win the class, which she did! He then told me to get on my horse and get ready for my pleasure class, which I did immediately. We laughed about that incident for years."

"Marvin and Marguerite taught me to ride when I was three years old. They taught me to love and to respect horses and dogs. I got in trouble a few times for running the horses too much and bringing them back lathered up. I was at the stable as much as I could be. It was a wonderful place to be, and I begged my mother to let me go.

"After I started school, Marguerite would pick me up, and I would ride during the week. I also rode on weekends. I was family, there was never a charge for me to ride. I spent many nights at Marvin and Marguerite's home at the rodeo grounds. Never once did I see Monty beaten nor even chastised. He and Larry often fought, as they were normal teenage brothers. They never seemed to get in much trouble for it. I thought Marvin and Marguerite were excellent parents. They could not have been more wonderful to me.

"They bought me all of my Western clothes and let me stay with them during the summer. Later when I was in high school, I lived with them when I competed for the California Rodeo Hostess title. I did not win the Hostess contest. I was All-County Cowgirl, however.

"During the Hostess contest, Marvin's horse, Sun Gown, balked and would not back up for me. I tried three or four times to get her to back, but she would not do it. I gently patted her neck and finished my performance. Marvin asked me what

happened. I told him about how I tried, but she would not respond. He got on her and checked it out, but he was as gentle with her as he had taught me to be."

1960s, MAKING A LIVING

Monty and Pat Roberts were at or near the end of their college years. Money was tight when an idea germinated and they got in touch with Marvin and Marguerite's good friends, the Garcias.

Henry and Angie had known Monty since he was a very young boy and wanted to help him in any way that they could. After much discussion, it was agreed that Monty and Pat would open a franchise to the Garcia Saddlery in San Luis Obispo. It looked like a win-win situation for everyone. Monty and Pat would operate the business that was earmarked for success.

The Garcias financed the store—right down to the postage stamps. Monty and Pat were given the keys and best wishes.

The Man Who Listens to Horses:

> While Pat was pursuing a diploma in business, we opened a shop to which we were able to give the famous "Garcia" name; the arrangement amounted to an early franchise operation. Garcia made the best Western equipment in North America, and our store was conveniently located between Cal Poly and the Proud Ranch. (p.106)

Interview with Skeeter Garcia Innocenti, Roberts student, 1998:

> *"My parents furnished a store for Monty and*

221

Pat in San Luis Obispo. It was stocked with merchandise, equipment, utilities, and my parents even provided the postage stamps to get them started. I don't think it cost Monty and Pat a single cent to get set up. Shortly after the store was opened, my parents began to get telephone calls from customers stating that they had stopped by the store, but it was closed.

"The store continued to lose money, and my parents couldn't afford to keep it stocked and pay the rent when no one was there to work. They told Monty and Pat that they would have to close it down, and Monty and Pat were very upset. My parents had little choice but to close the doors and wish Monty and Pat well."

EARLY 1960s

The Man Who Listens to Horses:

The economic climate for us appeared to brighten with the arrival of one Homer Mitchell. . . . The plan was that I help him build a [horse] training facility [near San Luis Obispo], which I would then manage for him. (p.107)

Monty established his horse training operation at Homer's eighty-acre ranch, called Laurellinda, and believed that with his reputation, his barn would soon be full of horses that were brought to him for training by paying customers.

When that didn't happen as planned, Monty says that he went to trainer Don Dodge for advice.

222

The Man Who Listens to Horses:

> We had given up our saddle-shop franchise now that our third baby was on the way. . . . someone said to me: "Go live with Don Dodge for a while." Don Dodge was possibly the most successful trainer of Western horses in the United States . . . . "If he believes in you, [it was said] you'll have it made. . . . (p.108)

Monty devotes eight pages of his book to an apprenticeship he says he had in Sacramento with noted horse trainer, Don Dodge. Under Don's direction, Monty asks readers to believe that he worked sixteen-hour days, had little to eat, and used his own meager resources to pay for a room in town. He claims that he took on a deathly pallor and was reduced to a skeleton while Don barked orders from the top of his lungs. To cap this absurd story, Don is supposed to have charged Monty thirty-two hundred dollars for the sixty-four day experience.

Don Dodge has been renowned as one of the nation's leading trainers of Western horses. His wins were impressive, his horses phenomenal, and his reputation solid. He did live and work for a time in Sacramento, California. Don knew Monty, having met him on the show circuit. The world of those who train champion Western performance horses is small. Anyone in that line of work will eventually meet and get to know others in the field. It's inevitable. They attend the same shows and compete for the same prize money.

Semiretired now, Don can still rattle off the names of horses he trained, the shows they attended, their wins, the years he showed them, their owner's names, and provide anyone willing to listen much more information than requested. He remembers Monty Roberts well. He also remembers Monty's father.

Interview with Don Dodge, Horse trainer, 1998:

"Marvin never showed much, but the boys did. Monty even showed a horse for me at the Cow Palace once. But that stuff in his book? Why that's just nonsense. Monty never worked for me, and I darn sure never charged him for givin' him any advice. He knows it and I know it.

"After his book came out and a lot of the people he talks about [in the book] started complainin' that it was not the truth, his wife Pat called me. She wanted to know if I was upset about what Monty had written about me.

"I said, 'No, Pat. I'm too old to be bothered by that kind of thing. But you and I know that none of it is true.'"

My Blue Heaven

Now lauded for his work with thoroughbreds and mustangs, Roberts spent many years working with performance horses.

The Man Who Listens to Horses:

[Joe Gray called me about a mare called My Blue Heaven. He was] worried for the safety of [his] daughters . . . At shows with one of his daughters in the saddle, she would apparently take the bit between her teeth, run away, and crash into fences or try to avoid fences by turning sharply and falling down at high speed. [He instructed me to sell the mare]. (pp.112, 113)

I decided to enter My Blue Heaven in a popular, high quality show . . . . [She won and] the family agreed that she should stay in training. . . . After I showed her for two seasons, she went on to compete under the two daughters successfully throughout the western United States. (pp.114, 115)

Interview with Joni Gray, Joe Gray's daughter, 1998:

"*My Blue Heaven never ran away with us, and we didn't want to sell her. She once belonged to Caroline Warner [Tugle] and was originally trained by Ralph and Vivian [Carter]. When Caroline went away to college, the mare remained at Carter's. Dad bought her for my sister Dot and me to show.*

"*We showed her for about a year at small shows and won trail, pleasure, and even some equitation classes. We went to Monty so that I could learn how to show a working cowhorse. I remember that Monty got excited about the mare because she was good at working cows. She wasn't so good at sliding to a stop.*

"*Monty talked my dad into letting him show the horse for us and Monty won a lot [of classes] with her. He put a nice stop her.*

"*It was after I left home for college that I learned what he did to her. I was told by someone that I consider an extremely reliable source, that Monty used a [piece of] wire on her bit to make her stop. Bits were not checked until after the cow work in those days. It was easy for him to have the wire pulled before he went back for the cow work [where he would] display a clean bit [for the judges].*"

After hearing this same story from several trusted sources, the disappointed Grays took My Blue Heaven home.

1962, Barlet

The Man Who Listens to Horses:

> Sometimes a horse comes along who is too troubled, too mean, to engage in conversation. (p.119)

> [Barlet] was too far gone to even ask for his trust. From a very young age he had been spoiled, not through cruelty in his case, but through unintended psychological abuse. He had been trained as a lapdog, and something had gone terribly wrong. (p.121)

> [After schooling] I was then able to show him in hand . . . . But he was never a mentally balanced horse after being spoiled as a foal. . . . he died in a fight with a gelding on my farm . . . . (p.121)

Monty claims that Marten Clark, who owned Barlet—a champion halter horse with outstanding conformation, found himself having to use an electric shock-wire around the horse's stall to keep from being attacked. Supposedly, Clark—another well-known and well-respected horseman—found it nearly impossible to show Barlet, so he offered Monty Roberts a one-half ownership of the colt if Monty could show him on halter and win. Barlet's value in 1962, says Monty, was in the neighborhood of thirty-five-thousand-dollars—a generous offer by Clark.

226

Interview with Marten Clark, Barlet's owner, 1998:

"None of that story that Monty wrote about my horse is true. I put the horse with Monty so he could show him. Monty is the one that wired the stall and said the horse was vicious. I never knew the horse to be vicious. He [Barlet] broke his leg while in Monty's care and had to be destroyed."

EARLY 1960s, HOSS DILDAY

Hoss Dilday is every bit the colorful character that the very sound of his name implies. Tempered some with age, he said he was honored to be included in the British version of Monty's book, but that some of Monty's details were incorrect.

Monty's version of the episode is simple and makes a cute story. Monty claims he was driving a new Oldsmobile and Hoss Dilday was riding shotgun, two of Monty's horses were in the trailer behind, and a Herb Alpert tape was playing when their engine caught fire near the small town of Huron, California.

The horses, trailer, tape, tack, Monty, and Hoss were saved, he says, but the car melted like a crispy marshmallow. Once they were rescued and back in the little valley town, it seems the only choices for accommodations were a brothel with a girl in every room or the local jail.

That's how Monty remembered his first night in a jail cell.

Interview with Hoss Dilday, Horse trainer, 1998:

"That's horse shit. Monty doesn't seem to remember much the way it really happened. Not

about that trip and not about how he used to train horses.

"It's a fact that car burned up, right down to the ground. I was the one drivin', and we sure as hell weren't listenin' to no Tijuana Brass. Johnny Tivio was the only horse in the trailer, and on top of that, we stayed in a Victorian boarding house. I even remember the name of the woman that owned it. It was Mrs. Hogan's hotel.

"Monty sure wasn't talkin' no Equus when I worked for him. He was always good showing a horse, but he preferred soap operas [on television], and that's where he usually was durin' the day.

"This is no secret; you can ask anybody who kept a horse there or took lessons from him. When Monty had a horse to discipline, he straightened it right up. I watched him use an axe handle on Barlet, and when Pay Gold wouldn't stop switchin' his tail, Monty put a piece of pipe under it and hit the top of it with a four-pound sledge hammer. Well, by God, that horse didn't switch his tail for a while."

Chapter 12

EARLY 1960S, LYNN ROBERTS

Lynn Roberts was an only child. Her early years began much as her father's before her: she first viewed the world from the back of a horse. Her parents, like her grandparents, kept a full stable. Her father, like her grandfather, believed horses and children were a good combination. She learned to ride from the best teachers, and horses were chosen for her as a way of life.

Larry and Patsy separated and divorced when their daughter, Lynn, was still very young. Consequently, Patsy raised Lynn with a great deal of assistance from Marvin and Marguerite after Larry left Salinas to pursue a life in Northern California. Lynn's mother worked hard to support herself and her young daughter. They remained loving members of the Roberts and the Martins families.

Lynn was a constant in her grandparent's life. Their loving care throughout her childhood was a godsend to Patsy, who relied on them to watch Lynn after school and during the long days of summer.

EARLY 1960S, CHERI RENEBOME

Pete and Joyce had lived in Redwood City when Cheryl Leigh, their third child, was born. That was in 1957. After his rodeo accident Pete took a job there with a company called Automotive Engineering, owned by his uncle, O. H. Day.

Pete hated working there but did his best. He had a family to feed, and he had made a commitment to his Uncle Ozzie. The job didn't last long though. Returning to Salinas after Cheri was born, Pete and Joyce settled once more in the community that would forever be known as *home,* no matter where they lived.

Pete had a good job and Joyce stayed home to raise the children, enrolling each in turn at Sacred Heart Elementary.

By the mid-1960s, they had saved enough to open a Ready Mix Concrete business. They were working hard, but they were happy, spending a lot of time with Joyce's family, especially Marguerite and Marvin.

1965, BUENA VISTA STABLES

Marvin Roberts was fifty-seven in 1965, when he and Marguerite purchased twenty-two acres of land off River Road, west of town. There, they set about creating a haven for horses and riders. Their modest home was neat and clean, decorated with Western memorabilia they had collected over the years. Too hot in the summer and cold in the winter, it was far from a mansion.

The two-bedroom bungalow sat unobtrusively on the side of the road like a worn visage of the depressed 1930s. Inside, it overflowed with a warm and loving atmosphere, and the aroma of Marguerite's great cooking.

Vehicles whizzed by on River Road at fifty, sixty, and seventy miles an hour. Each one caused the windows to rattle in their casings as the vibrating tremors moved out from the surface of the road to the foundation of the house. Behind the house, barns, and corrals, was the unpredictable and ever-changing Salinas River.

About two hundred yards separated Marvin and Marguerite from their closest neighbors, the Massolos. In that space between the two houses, sitting on low ground between the river and the levy road, were the horse stalls. Here, among the cottonwoods and cattails, the Roberts established the riding and boarding stables they would call home for their final twenty years of life.

The single row of box stalls was built from an old labor camp building. The camp was dismantled, board by board, and the lumber used to build stalls and a tack room with a small office at one end. Dutch Hoffmann, a neighbor and friend, helped Marvin with much of the work. Another friend, Alan Balch, pitched in as a gofer.

When the barn was up and the steep corrugated tin roof in place, Marvin put up the sign. It was made of large block letters, each about two feet tall, painted red, that proudly proclaimed Buena Vista Stables from the barn's roof. Marvin was so very proud of that sign.

The place wasn't fancy, but it was theirs. For the first time in their lives, Marvin and Marguerite owned a piece of real property—twenty-two acres of it.

Letter from Audrie Massolo Waltrip, River Road neighbor, 1998:

"The Massolo family has owned land on River Road since nineteen twenty-nine. What an honor to learn the Roberts would build a stable on the property adjacent to us.

"Marvin and Marguerite turned it into a center for fun. They built the stables and worked hard to make it a success. I remember kids being dropped off early in the morning and picked up late in the evenings.

"My parents worked and ran a vegetable stand next door; we called it God's Little Acres. When I was a child, my brother and I helped clean and clear the property at our place and later we planted and hoed weeds and then picked

231

vegetables. It was hard work, but we did it as a family and as friends.

"We did it because we loved our parents. They didn't beat us into submission. I was not so lucky to be able to ride at Marvin and Marguerite's. I wanted to, but work came first. My children, Billy and Mindy, were the ones who learned to ride by watching and then getting lessons after they did their chores at the ranch.

"More people these days would love to raise their kids that way—working as a family. My mother and father had other jobs as well. They both worked in the lettuce sheds and later drove lettuce trucks, all the while operating our small vegetable truck farm on River Road. My parents, like Marvin and Marguerite, had few vacations. Perhaps that is why the two neighbors got along so well. They didn't have time for coffee klatches."

The deep sandy soil of the river bottom was great for the horse's legs. The many cottonwood trees offered shade and a wooded area for exploring. A new generation of riders loved it there. With an always-changing view provided by nature, it was a fascinating place to ride, investigate new trails, and get better acquainted with a four-legged friend.

Without fences to delineate property lines, it afforded much more than the twenty-two acres Marvin and Marguerite had purchased. Until it flooded.

Interview with Cheri Renebome Little, Robert's niece, Joyce's daughter, 1996:

"I was nine, and I remember it like yesterday. We went out to help Uncle Marvin and Aunt Marguerite evacuate because the river was rising fast! Uncle Marvin and the men got the horses to high ground and safety with the neighbors. We got what we could out of the house, and then we waited.

"I remember seeing the chickens lined up on top of the barn, and that was all you could see of the barn—just the roof with chickens hanging on for dear life. We later went to Pedrazzi's on the high side of the road and camped out. It was like a big party. I remember all the women fixed a big breakfast for everyone the next day.

"When the river receded, Marvin and Marguerite were left with a giant mess of black gook!

"Uncle Marvin and Aunt Marguerite were to endure two or three more floods after that. They

BUENA VISTA STABLES

233

were survivors. Even with all that was going on, I never remember either of them taking it out on anyone around them. They just mucked up and kept on working. Marvin would put all the harness leather and other equipment in barrels of oil to undo the damage of the river. It was really an awful mess."

When nature struck a wicked blow to the Buena Vista Stables, she left a trail of broken trees and debris: unidentifiable pieces of other lives she had stolen from upriver. The mud, however, was her crowning revenge. Thick, soft, and black, she spread it softly over everything that dared to steal a corner of her wide bed. Finally satisfied that no challengers would take her throne; her waters began to recede. Left behind, was the rich, black mud—a memento of her interminable power.

For centuries past and centuries to come, the river remains. Three times, she took from Marvin and Marguerite a toll for using the land she would always reclaim. Three times, they evacuated horses, saddles, and equipment. Three times, they raced to move their possessions to safety. Three times, they repaired damaged buildings, repainted interior and exterior walls. Three times, the little house managed to cling to a small patch of solid earth as the river first lapped at the back porch and finally forced its way in, uninvited, to deposit a rich layer of silt that only a shovel could later remove.

Three times, Marvin and Marguerite were reminded that no possession was greater than that of friends and family. Friends they knew well and friends they had never known arrived in pickup trucks and cattle trucks. They came with horse trailers, stock trailers, flatbeds, and tractors. They came to help.

Interview with Alan Balch, friend and student, 1997:

"Along with the good times were the bad. At least twice, the Salinas River flooded. Horses, saddles, tack, and household possessions had to be moved. Neighbors and others came to their aid. Among them were the Hoffmanns, Grecos, Massolos, Pedrazzis, Renebomes, and the Victorinis. I don't believe Marvin ever got rid of anything, as I remember moving much of the same stuff time and time again. But the river, I guess, took some items away."

It usually took a week or so for the river to recede. Without fail, that's when friends returned with shovels, soap, disinfectant, rags, and paintbrushes. There was work to be done.

It was not an easy life. By most standards, it was a hard existence. "Life does not always send us down the easy road," Marguerite said one day as she surveyed the flood ravaged arena. "I guess that's why you gotta make darn sure you like what you're doin' with it," she laughed. "Come on, we'll have a lesson over on drier ground behind Massolo's."

Late 1960s, The Next Generation

Interview with Syd Auker, Roberts student, 1997:

"After I had taken several lessons from the Roberts, Marvin helped my parents find a horse for me in nineteen sixty-three. They purchased Tammy for my tenth birthday. I can still see her tied to a big tree in front of the Roberts house.

She wore a big red bow and a sign that read, 'Happy Birthday Sydney, Love, Tammy.'

"Growing up at the Roberts stables was great fun. At Buena Vista we had so much property around us that it felt like heaven. There was land and water all around for us to explore. Boy did we have fun doing just that. Of course, with the fun came work. Before we could play, we had to work. They taught us that horsemanship and horse care came first, then cool down, then fun, but not too much fun.

"Marguerite always stressed safety. I'm sure she had her hands full with so many kids running around. I can still hear her yell, yes, yell, from her kitchen window, 'You're cruising for a bruising!' Since I don't remember many accidents, we must have heeded her warnings.

"Most of us belonged to the Monterey County Junior Horsemen's Association and attended monthly meetings at the Roberts house. The club was all about promoting horses and fun for us. We took day rides into the hills, to the beach, to horse shows and, of course, we rode in California Rodeo parade every year. To me, Big Week was the best. Marvin and Marguerite coordinated it all for us.

"We took our horses to the rodeo grounds and boarded them there for the entire four days of the rodeo. Many of us showed our horses in various classes there too. Marvin and Marguerite set everything up for the entire four days. It seems *like our only task in preparation was to ride from the stables by the river to the rodeo grounds.*

"Even that was fun. The day before the rodeo got underway everyone from the stables rode to town with Marvin. After four days of our great rodeo, all the kids went home to collapse while Marvin and Marguerite loaded our horses, hauled them back to the stables, and then tended to the many chores they still had to do.

"One thing that amazes me, as I think about it, is how incredibly much they did for us. My parents just dropped me off at the stables. It was always the Roberts who got us to whatever destination we had selected for a special ride or whatever horse show we were going to attend.

"I remember when we had beach rides. Marvin would get up very early to trailer all the horses to Moss Landing Beach. He had to make several trips. Again, all we did was show up and have fun!

"I recently asked my parents about fees

Marguerite judging horsemanship.

237

charged for all these extra activities and they replied, 'Nothing.'

"They told me that the only money Marvin and Marguerite asked for besides the monthly board for Tammy was for horseshoeing. Marvin was always working with the kids and their horses, helping with any riding problems. He never charged us for those lessons. He just wanted us to be better horsemen and women. Besides that, Marvin and Marguerite just wanted us to be better people.

"I think of what it costs for my daughter to ride now, and I can't believe all that they gave to us without charge. But then again, I'm speaking of Marvin and Marguerite Roberts. They did these things for kids to help teach great horsemanship and great lessons to use in life. I will never forget those lessons or my time with them."

Interview with Lynn Granger Aebi, Roberts student, 1997:

"In the fall of nineteen sixty-eight, I was an eight-year-old girl hopelessly lovesick for horses. My father introduced me to a man named Marvin Roberts. Unknown to me at the time, this man and his wife Marguerite were to have an incredible influence on my life. Marvin and Marguerite owned the Buena Vista Stables, located along the Salinas River. They opened their door and their hearts to young people of all ages.

"Marvin taught me how to ride on an old

238

lesson horse named Gypsy. In the beginning, Marvin rode behind me. He helped me gain balance, as well as confidence. As time went on and I progressed, Marvin would stand in the center of the arena or ride a young horse that he was training during my lessons.

"After a few months, my dad bought me a young quarter horse named Snoopy. This horse had a wild streak in him, and I had to learn to ride or die trying. Marvin had the patience of Job working with a green rider on a green horse. We were soon progressing rapidly.

"The things I learned at the Buena Vista Stables went way beyond learning to manage and ride a young horse. I learned about giving to others and sharing time with a person in need of help, even when there might be one thousand other things to be done. I learned to respect and care for my horse and countless other positive life skills.

"At the stables, Marvin and Marguerite would always stop what they were doing to help the kids out. We would beg Marguerite to school us prior to a horse show, because she was tough as nails, and we knew we would get quality instruction. Marvin would constantly stop his work to teach us something new, from riding to clipping, horse care to the care of our riding equipment.

"I spent many days at the Buena Vista Stables during the summers in the late nineteen sixties. I remember Marvin as a man who loved animals and people alike, especially children. He was one

of the most giving and unselfish men I have ever met.

"Marvin and Marguerite were real quality human beings and I feel this world would be much better if we had more people like them living in it.

"I will never forget the Roberts and the life skills they helped to instill in me. As the mother of a ten-year-old girl, I wish we had a Buena Vista Stables nearby."

LATE 1960S, THE FLAG IS UP

The salty Pacific is rolling north as it laps the California coast at Santa Barbara. Dipping a graceful hip in the sea, the city contentedly curls below the protective mountains to the north and basks in the warmth of her clever exposure to the sun. Santa Barbara is a feminine city.

A gull catches a current of cool air and glides inland across the strand. Artists and street vendors are poised to catch tourists; blue paint on white canvas squares carry bold signatures and expensive price tags. Kiosks that might offer T-shirts and beads in another city, are stocked here with Chanel knockoffs, Gucci sunglasses, and hand-painted designs on silk shirts.

Santa Barbara is proud and confident. She is strong and independent. She displays her heritage as proudly as a woman with a three-karat diamond ring. And yes, there are a lot of three-karat diamond rings in Santa Barbara.

White stucco walls of the forties and fifties are now painted ecru, sand, or another hue of soft beige and tan. A few of the red tile roofs are still in place, though most

240

are now a terra cotta orange. The heavy oak beamed porticos and bright tile frescos, palm trees, fountains, gardens, and street names like Anapamu and Salsipuedes give Santa Barbara her charm and distinctive flavor. All of this, she cradles in beautiful Spanish arms.

The travel brochures say Santa Barbara is a city with something for everyone and every price range, a city rich in culture and water sports. Her restaurants, resorts, and wineries are treasures to be discovered and savored. She accepts the growing popularity of fast food restaurants as a nuisance to be tolerated.

To the east, beyond the suburbs of Montecito and Summerland, Highway 101 turns south through Ventura and Oxnard. Along marshy flats and rugged mountains, like a river on a steady course, 101 reaches the sea of asphalt seas, Los Angeles, and loses the distinctive characteristics that made it special along the coast. A U-turn is recommended.

In the opposite direction, slicing west across ridges and valleys, the highway follows the only east-west stretch of Pacific coastline from Alaska to Cape Horn. Turning north at Gaviota Pass, children on family vacations strain against seat belts to see, and dads delight them with the automobile horn's echo as they drive through the short mountain tunnel and emerge unscathed.

Inland, the Santa Ynez Mountains are covered with the lush growth of manzanita, eucalyptus, pine, and oak. A rich and nubby green blanket that drops to the valley as if falling from giant knees propped on the earth. Less than an hour from Santa Barbara, lie the sheltered communities of Buellton, Santa Ynez, and Solvang—unlikely triplets amid the micro valleys of vineyards, wineries, and horse farms. It was here that wealthy publishing magnate Hastings Harcourt and horse trainer Monty Roberts built a dream.

Harcourt had no idea in 1966 that his dream would become a nightmare or that he could have been so wrong in his judgement of character.

Around 1964, while Monty was training horses at Homer Mitchell's Laurellinda Ranch, he met the millionaire Hastings Harcourt. Standing over six-feet tall with broad shoulders and dark hair that was beginning to thin, Harcourt's impeccable attire and commanding physique marked him a man of distinction. He wore heavy horn-rimmed glasses, popular at the time, and his friends described him as kind, generous, and often too trusting for a man of his financial position.

Harcourt was enchanted with Monty's eloquent manner and obvious talent with horses. He asked Roberts to train a quarter horse colt he had purchased as a gift for his son. Monty did such a good job that the colt placed fourth in a field of fifty competitors in the Channel City Horse Show at Santa Barbara. Harcourt was impressed. Monty was gaining his favor and his trust.

By 1966, Harcourt was so taken with Roberts that he made plans to create a premiere thoroughbred farm and make Monty his managing partner. From the beginning, Hastings believed in his plan. Sophisticated, worldly, and intelligent, Hastings Harcourt had vision. Monty Roberts had knowledge and talent. Together they would make that vision a profitable reality.

If the thousands of dollars that Homer Mitchell spent on Laurallinda allowed Monty and Pat to start making a living with horses, Harcourt's millions could catapult the couple into equine industry stardom.

Monty's vision was rolling in Technicolor when he said good-bye to Homer.

Harcourt and Monty Roberts formed a partnership. Trusting the charismatic horse trainer, Harcourt gave Monty a loose rein to build a thoroughbred breeding and training facility near Solvang, California. They named it Flag Is Up Farms, and Monty oversaw construction using Harcourt's nearly unlimited budget to create the world-class operation.

Monty moved his family into the beautiful home overlooking the farm in 1967. Wardrobes were purchased; art collected; nannies, housekeepers, and cooks hired. Air travel across the continent and the Atlantic became frequent. It was an auspicious lifestyle for Monty's young family.

Monty Roberts was entrusted with the facility and multimillion dollar decisions regarding the acquisition and disposition of bloodstock. His contract included additional earnings he could make. Hastings Harcourt was satisfied the farm would someday turn a profit. He thought of Monty as a son and blindly assumed that his generosity would assure loyalty.

The stage had been set. The props were magnificent. The conductor was resplendent when he donned his new tweed cap.

Along with the many thoroughbreds that passed through Monty's barns, there were several quarter horses as well: horses that Monty trained for others and horses of his own.

The true and complete account of events that took place in the lives of Monty Roberts and Hasting Harcourt between 1966 and 1976 could fill the pages of a best-seller. Most of the people who know the intimate details are silenced. Death, court orders, and laws of attorney-client privilege have helped keep Truth buried.

While elegantly surrounded by rich green pastures, tree-lined driveways, and sleek thoroughbred horses, millions of dollars were lost, relationships and trusts were destroyed, and reputations were damaged. The unconscionable details have no place in this book, except to clear misconceptions about individuals that Monty Roberts publicly maligned.

The Man Who Listens to Horses:
Harcourt [has] "sand-castle syndrome": [like a] child on the beach [he takes] as much joy in destruction as in creation. . . . we had built a sand-castle for Hastings Harcourt. (p.131)

[Harcourt said,] "I must sell the farm . . . ." [He] was heading into free fall. (p.132) . . . [I was then instructed to kill five horses.] (pp.133, 134) There was no time to feel sorry for myself . . . if I failed to move quickly, things would be taken out of my hands. (p.134)

"You're under arrest, [we're] acting on a complaint that you've stolen two million dollars and that you're about to flee the country." (p.138) . . . I filed a wrongful prosecution suit against Harcourt for $30 million. (p.142) . . . The compensation paid to us by Harcourt allowed us to buy the farm. (p.143)

1972–1976, THE FLAG IS UP
Early in 1972, Monty Roberts was arrested and put in jail. Hastings Harcourt alleged that Monty Roberts

breached a fiduciary relationship with him, that he acted with the intent to deceive and defraud, and that he conspired to deceive and defraud. Resulting from the deceit and fraud, Harcourt alleged he had been financially damaged.

The evidence against Monty, which is part of the public record in those proceedings, is overwhelming. In the formal complaint filed in the Superior Court of the State of California, derivatives of the words "deceit and fraud" appear no less than fourteen times.

Though Monty was under a contractual agreement with Harcourt that included a fiduciary relationship, the compliant contends that Monty misrepresented the dollar amount on several business transactions. Actual sums Monty received, acting ostensibly for Harcourt, appeared to have been converted for his own benefit.

The names of numerous horses and dollar amounts are included in the complaint.

To his family and friends, Monty said it was a giant misunderstanding. He filed a wrongful prosecution suit against Harcourt for thirty-million-dollars.

For twenty-five years, Monty's family in Salinas believed that he gained title to the farm in an out-of-court settlement with Harcourt. However, court records, property deeds, and other documents do not support that assumption.

Searching for answers to a twenty-five-year-old question seemed impossible. The trail was cold and carefully covered. Countless hours were spent at the Santa Barbara County courthouse and on the telephone. A bit of information here led to a contact there. Interviews with those connected to Monty during the Harcourt years took on the same general hue. The emerging portrait was dark and ugly.

Pieced together bit by bit, the accumulated evidence shows that in the end Harcourt walked away from confrontation and allowed Monty to plead *nolo contendere* to a lesser charge. Harcourt then sold the farm to a group of investors and tried to get on with his life.

Why? Why would Hastings Harcourt walk away? There was strong physical evidence that Monty had been dishonest in his dealings with Harcourt. Why would he let Monty plead to a reduced charge?

Whispered rumors were tracked, paper trails were followed, and statements were taken. Eyes welled with tears, and slowly an ugly portrait was bared to those who dared to look beneath the surface.

Harcourt's dream evaporated like the trust he had placed in Monty and Pat. He prayed it would be over—a nightmare from which to wake.

Quietly, though, the players were changing sets on the darkened stage. The property's ownership moved through several unseen hands. New names went on the land's title. Quitclaim deeds were filed. The names kept changing. The tweed cap was back in the barns in a year.

Monty leads readers to believe that he was arrested, in part, because he tried to save the lives of five horses that Harcourt ordered, through his emissary, to be killed. Monty said it was Harcourt's desire to destroy Flag Is Up Farms and all they had built together.

Horrified readers found sympathy for Monty. Obviously, they said, he did the right thing. He saved the horses, did he not? What could be more important? Their adoration grew as they envisioned his compassion and gentle manner.

How can the truth be such an elusive enigma?

Truth: There were no horses to save. There were no orders for Monty to kill any horses or anything else.

Monty did not purchase Flag Is Up Farm with compensation paid to him by Harcourt.

The nameless emissary in the United States edition of *The Man Who Listens to Horses* is named in the United Kingdom edition. He was interviewed in 1998.

Interview with Harcourt's associate whom Monty says ordered him to kill five horses, 1998:

"None of the horses [at Flag Is Up Farms] were ever ordered to be put down. I love animals. I own four dogs and could never have done what Monty suggests that I did.

"Hastings loved Monty and Pat and treated them like family, losing millions in the process. The first I heard of Monty's idiotic claim about destroying the horses and farm was in his book.

"Hastings did not try to destroy the farm."

Several people who were close to Hastings Harcourt during the ordeal confirmed the statement that Harcourt had loved Monty as a son. Harcourt's personal assistant and his personal pilot were among those who could not believe that Harcourt would order any horse to be killed. They also refuse to believe that Hastings suffered from any sand-castle syndrome, bipolar disease, or any other mental debilitation, as Monty suggests.

When the curtain finally dropped on the whole ugly ordeal, and the credits rolled, the conductor, resplendent in his trademark tweed cap, figuratively bowed to a standing ovation from his many minions.

By the time *The Man Who Listens to Horses* was in print, Monty and Pat owned Flag Is Up Farms. A perfect near-ending to a near-perfect plan. All that could make it better was to make it tax exempt.

Soon thereafter, the Monty Roberts World Learning Center was developed.

Hastings Harcourt is dead. The investors of the 1970s are gone. The tweed cap of Monty Roberts remains. The farm stands proudly. The horses stand quietly. Life goes on. Whispers and lies circulate the globe. Monty is applauded. His family, friends, and those who know the truth are sickened.

When this book went to print, there was no information available regarding the tax status of Monty and Pat Roberts or the Flag Is Up Farms.

1972, BUFFALO BABCOCK

Monty told a whale of a tale regarding his 1972 incarceration in the Santa Barbara county jail that credits his own extraordinary ability. It seems that a man named Buffalo Babcock shared Monty's jail cell there. The story validates Monty's quick wit but does little to reaffirm his self-described *gentle* manner.

The Man Who Listens to Horses:

[They had] a murderer waiting in a cell . . . to convince [me] to plead guilty. (p.138) I was introduced to Buffalo Babcock. . . . [He] looked like a cross between a grizzly and Bigfoot. . . . I was shackled to him, face-to-face through a floating ring, with heavy metal collars at our wrists and ankles. An **X** formed between us. . . . The deal was this: He would convince me, nicely or not, to plead guilty and thus win for himself a dismissal of charges. (p.139)

I was quick and strong. . . . I hoisted the chain around his ankles and he came crashing down, banging his head on the corner of the iron bunk. . . . several hundred prisoners were yelling and applauding . . . . I was a hero for vanquishing Babcock . . . (p.140)

There is no record of any Babcock, Buffalo or otherwise, in the Santa Barbara County jail at the time. No record could be found of anyone, by any name, booked in the jail for murder, attempted murder, or shooting a jukebox at the time Monty was a guest there.

SPEAKING OF BUFFALO(ED)

In the forward to *The Man Who Listens to Horses*, Lawrence Scanlan writes:

"The American military heard about Monty's unusual skill and wanted him to fly as a passenger in a spy plane over enemy territory during the Korean war: with his eyes he would not be duped by camouflage. Monty declined. (p.xxiv)"

Remember that Monty was born in 1935. North Korea invaded South Korea on June 25, 1950, this was the beginning of the Korean War. Monty had just turned fifteen years old. On June 27, 1953, President Dwight D. Eisenhower was instrumental in negotiating an armistice to end the Korean War. Monty was eighteen years old and had just graduated from high school.

The Man Who Listens to Horses:
> Mine is a rare [vision] condition, quite separate from the more common one in which an individual cannot properly distinguish colors.
>
> When I was young, no one believed that I could see only in black and white, but I have subsequently learned that I see in a way very different from normally sighted people. (p. 21)

Monty also claims that he could see clearly for quite a distance at night. He describes a man who could read a license plate four blocks away. His family and others knew Monty as color-blind, but none heard that he saw only in black and white or that he had acute night vision.

Two optometrists said they had never heard of the combined black-and-white-with-acute-sight condition Monty describes. Neither of the eye doctors were aware of a human being with strictly black and white vision, but believed it was possible.

None of Monty's friends or family were aware that he was wanted by the military.

Forty-Seven Children?

Lawrence Scanlan writes in the Afterword:
> Over time, Pat and Monty took in forty-seven children, some staying for years and living like brothers and sisters to Deborah and Laurel and Marty.(p.242)
>
> By Monty's reckoning, every one of those forty-seven children had cause to falter. . . . Most came from dysfunctional families. Here were nestlings with broken wings, but—again by Monty's own

250

reckoning—forty of them learned to fly . . . . The rest landed in jail or returned to the streets and died there. Their fates were distressing blows to Monty and Pat, but he argues that . . . their overall outcome reflects well on his approach. And it is his approach that Monty wants the world to consider.(p.243)

Monty says his approach with horses works with humans and implies that he has a forty out of forty-seven success record to prove it. On video, two of these alleged children praise Monty's work. Unable to reach the two, contact was made with a third name given by Roberts: Bruno DeBerdt.

In the late 1960s, Bruno lived near Salinas and rode at the Buena Vista Stables. He was a boy in love with horses and spoke of becoming a jockey. Marvin, as he did so often for others, provided an opportunity for Bruno; a jockey apprenticeship with Monty. With Marvin's recommendation, Bruno's parents let him move to the Flag Is Up Farms.

Quoted by Ronna Snyder in the February, 1999, issue of *Horse and Rider*, Bruno said, "I wasn't a foster child." Monty and Pat reminded Bruno that he had lived on their property, they had been responsible for his welfare, and that he had, after all, been their foster child.

Bruno is now an international equine shipping agent who still does business with Monty and Pat. He has since signed a letter stating that he was their foster child.

Dean Anders, former teacher, principal, and superintendent with the Santa Ynez Valley High School District for thirty-seven years, said that he could not recall a single child enrolled by Monty Roberts, other than his three biological children, though any foster child would have been required to attend school.

Cheri Little spent a childhood summer with her cousins, Deborah, Laurel, and Marty. She wonders if her name is listed among the forty-seven. After all, she surmised, she had lived on their property for several weeks, and Monty and Pat had made decisions regarding her welfare during that time.

Chapter 13

1971, BUENA VISTA STABLES

The sweet stench from the Spreckles sugar factory permeated the air. Several students were already in the arena or out on trails. The missing saddles indicated a busy day.

There might have been seven or eight riders with Marvin in the arena. Most of those who rode with Marvin and Marguerite at the Buena Vista Stables rode Western, that is, using a Western saddle and tack. Not only is the equipment different from the lightweight English saddle, the riding styles vary as well. Marvin was schooling a young quarter horse mare called Debbie Twist.

The students were much like basketball players during the warm-up session. Each rider, keenly aware of his or her own particular problem area, worked to improve before the imminent arrival of the coach, Marguerite.

"Are you about ready out there?" she bellowed from the porch overlooking the arena. No one knew how she did it, but Marguerite seemed to have eyes in the back of her head. She seemed to know exactly what was going on at all times. It came from experience. The students in the 1970s were not much different from the students she'd had in the 1960s, '50s, '40s, or even the '30s.

It's said that timing is everything. Marguerite's timing was impeccable. Whether her voice was raised to chastise or softened to console, she knew exactly how to add impact to her voice.

At the sound of that voice, the horses' ears shot forward, riders reined up, and everyone focused on the dark-haired woman making her way down the hill. It was time to go to work. Though most of those who kept a horse at the stables paid only boarding fees, these incredible people continued to offer guidance and lessons on a regular basis. Always free of any additional charge.

The remarkable phenomenon of Marvin and Marguerite may not be the indelible imprint they made on the lives of so many but rather that they did it continually, for more than fifty years. When their peers were traveling on cruise ships or visiting great grandchildren, the Roberts were in the arena.

Marguerite positioned herself in the center of the arena and the riders circled like moths around a bare bulb in the dark. She watched in silence as they took to the rail at a walk, moving to the left. Each one praying not to be chastised first. Someone would be; someone had to be. Once she assessed the group, the instructions would begin. Her favorites were: "Chin up and heels down." Particularly hated was, "Bring those elbows in to your sides; you look like a chicken trying to fly." Marguerite knew it worked. Elbows sucked in and stayed glued to the sides of the riders in training. During group lessons, it did not matter that an admonishment was issued to a particular individual. When the group heard a reprimand, each strived to improve.

Her goal was to make better riders. Whether she was standing in the arena or looking out the kitchen window, if Marguerite saw a problem, she asserted herself and instructed the rider to correct the error.

Concentration counts. Whether riding a horse, playing golf, or taking the heart-stopping, three-point shot to the hoop in the final seconds of a championship basketball game, without concentration on doing it right, the results often fall short of perfection and the win goes to someone else.

How often has it been said, "Oh, sorry, I wasn't paying attention."

Marvin and Marguerite taught their students to pay attention. They taught them to take that philosophy of concentration on doing it right and apply it to their daily lives. It's no wonder those students credit the Roberts for teaching life skills that made them winners.

"Reverse at the walk," she instructed and the group simultaneously turned to the center of the ring and began to circle to the right.

"Lope your horses," she called once all were moving nicely to the right. She then focused on each horse and rider for an instant as she determined whether everyone was on the correct lead.

When taking a horse from a walk to a lope or canter, the objective is not to simply speed up. A lope is a three-beat gait characterized by the extension of either the left or right leg ahead of the opposite side. These are called leads. If the legs on the right side are extending ahead of the left, the horse is on his right lead. If the legs on the left side are extending ahead of the right, the horse is on his left lead. The correct lead is always the one leading in the same direction that the horse is moving. Circle to the right: right lead. It is imperative in the show ring to position your horse on the correct lead to accommodate the direction he is headed.

Two horses picked up the wrong leads. One rider quickly worked to correct the problem while the other continued to gallop oblivious to any problem.

"Doesn't that ride feel rough, Cathy?"

The young rider realized her mistake. Marguerite helped her put the horse on lead then turned her attention to the rest.

"By now, all of you should be able to feel your leads. If you can't, look at your horse's shoulder without moving your head," she said. "With your eyes only, I want you to determine your lead. I know you can do it if you try," she added.

Working his young filly in the arena with the students, Marvin would ride by and offer a quiet but encouraging word or a suggestion for improvement to each as he passed.

Marguerite gave a forty-five minute workout then told the students to cool the horses and let them relax. "Go for a nice walk now, and don't you be runnin' those horses," she warned, just in case anyone might be thinking that a run along the river sounded like fun.

Of course it was fun. Once the fear is gone, the feel of riding a powerful horse surging forward over the sand and knifing through the wind is as romantic as it sounds. This horse, this noble being, is much like a child. To run free and play can be wondrous fun, but when it is earned as a reward after lessons, the value increases.

It can be a painful lesson to learn the hard way that a horse is not a machine. He is a living, breathing animal. Like other great athletes, he needs warm up and cool down time. The importance of that cannot be over stressed. He must build his strength and stamina over time. Like an athlete works and conditions his muscles at the gym, so the handler must condition his horse.

Another valuable lesson learned at the stables was that dedication to work earns freedom to play. With freedom comes responsibility. Anyone who owns or rides a horse has the responsibility to give it the very best of care. That care doesn't stop at feeding and grooming. That care includes an exercise program, health care, and training.

Nearly everyone who boarded a horse at Buena Vista spent the weekend and all day on both Saturday and Sunday at the stables. In summertime, it might have been easier to set up cots in the tack room. No one wanted to go home.

During daylight hours, someone was always around. If it was raining, everyone sat in the tack room and played Crazy-8s or Go Fish. A deck of cards was always handy for emergency weather conditions. Besides, the horses did need rest periods. Six-, seven-, and eight-hour days were normal for most of the Roberts students. Days were spent riding some, working some, playing some, and enjoying their friends and the horses.

The four o'clock whistle that blew at the sugar factory was usually the cue to head toward the barn. Most parents dropped their offspring at the stables around nine in the morning and returned by five or six to pick them up. By then, the horses were ready for dinner.

The distinctive sound of Marvin's boots and spurs as he shuffled across the wooden porch meant he was on his way back to the barn. The years of riding and hard work had taken a toll on his joints.

With a pocketful of carrots, he gently pulled one out and fed it to a mare at the hitching rail. He rubbed her forehead, and she rubbed back. From the twinkle in his eye, this ritual had been played more than once. The bond between them was unmistakable. The carrot may have been a treat, but this mare was smitten with Marvin.

"She loves these carrots," he said with a wink. "A' course, they all do." He waved an arm toward the bank of stalls.

Ten horses stood with necks arched toward Marvin, their heads bobbing up and down over the stall doors as they called to him with gentle nickering. Their version of a horse whisper—telling Marvin they were ready for dinner and hoped for a carrot too.

It had been a long day, a good day. It was a day much like the one before and the one to follow. It was a day for students to reflect on lessons, horses, and each other. Their relationships with horses were very much like their relationships with humans. It was usually to a horse that a student first told their dreams, fears, loves, and desires. It was often the horse that they cried with, laughed with, and shared secret thoughts with. The horses were their best friends, and they never betrayed one another.

The riders who trained in April 1971 were like riders who had trained with Marvin and Marguerite since the 1930s: none were forced to attend. All were commanded to learn. Marvin and Marguerite would have it no other way. Learn first, then have fun. Students learned some and played some every single day under their guidance.

It was not just humans that learned from Marvin and Marguerite, the horses learned too. They learned purpose. They had a job. Rather than hang out at the corner pasture with the herd, they went to work and were paid extra for their efforts, especially the horses that entered the show ring. Blankets, warm stalls in the winter, a pedicure every six weeks, round-the-clock health care if needed, and best of all, extra grain.

For twenty years, Marvin and Marguerite ran The Buena Vista Stables on River Road. The number of students dwindled as the years wore on, but Marvin and Marguerite's dedication never wavered.

THE RACE IS ON

Marvin also liked to dabble a bit in horse racing. Too big to be a jockey, he used his keen eye and good horse sense to spot a potential winner. When he did, he'd scout a suitable rider, train the two together, and grin like Jimmy Carter if his students were successful.

Interview with Pete Renebome, Joyce's husband, 1996:

"A story comes to mind that I think shows the character of Marvin.

"Joyce and I stopped by the Roberts for a visit as we often did on weekends. Our children would ride while we were there, and we would visit. On this particular occasion, Marvin stopped me before I got to the door. He asked me to come and look at an Arabian horse he had in training.

"'Sahara and you will make a great entry in an endurance race scheduled to run along the river from King City to Greenfield. It's less than fifteen miles long,' he said with a twinkle in his eye. 'What do ya say, Pete?'

"The race was a month away, and I was to train and work with the horse every Sunday for the rest of the month until the day of the big race. Marvin would ride him during the week to keep him conditioned. It wasn't much time but it sounded like something we would enjoy.

"I admit I got a little nervous when we arrived at the staging area and saw all the fancy-looking

horses there. *A lot of the fellows were trying to wager bets against us. Marvin wasn't about to get suckered into betting. He told the guys that Sahara and I had only been in training for a short while and he didn't expect miracles. Soon after the bets were placed among the crowd, the race got underway.*

"Marvin and the other drivers followed the race by driving along the edge of the highway to make sure everything went okay. About halfway to Greenfield, I knew Sahara and I had had enough. He was lathered up pretty heavy, and his breathing was labored. I got off and led him out of the riverbed. Marvin spotted us with the binoculars and drove over to meet us.

"Sahara and I scrambled up the bank and made our way toward Marvin who carried a cooling sheet for Sahara and water for me. I was concerned he'd be upset because we didn't finish the race. Marvin showed me again the kind of man he was when he said to me, 'You did the right thing, Pete. No race is worth a horse's life.'

"Marvin was a man of honor. In the thirty-four years that I knew him, we never once had harsh words between us. He and Marguerite were very special people in our lives and in the lives of our children."

EARLY 1970S, SANTA BARBARA COUNTY

In Santa Barbara County there is an exclusive and elite organization known as Los Rancheros Vistadores. Membership is by invitation only and includes the areas most respected individuals. A somewhat secret society for "men only" they meet annually to ride the land of their ancestors, barbecue great slabs of steaks, eat, drink, and in short, have a good time. To be included among the rank and file of the Vistadores is an honor among the horsemen, cattle ranchers, landowners, and celebrities of the Pacific Southwest.

Monty Roberts is no longer welcome. His exclusion stemmed from an incident that few will discuss. Membership requires an oath. No member may discuss the behavior of another member or guest to anyone at anytime. The premise being that within the confines of the Los Rancheros Vistadores, a man can be himself, free to do the manly things he might not choose to do in public. He can eat too much, drink too much, and act a fool if he so desires. Their annual ride is a time of laughter, camaraderie, and youthful pranks.

In any society, secret or not, there are those rare events that so shock and outrage that a mere mortal cannot control his wagging tongue. More than one member of the Vistadores shared the details of an incident that occurred more than twenty years ago—after which Monty was reputedly asked never to return.

Horse racing has long been a favorite sport of gentlemen. The Vistadores discovered that mule racing was also great fun. With a remuda of mules at their camp in the mountains, the adventurous men chose their mounts and placed their bets. The wagers were considerable, reaching four figures. The race was on.

261

The first two riders neared the finish line as the men shouted and cheered. But the crowd's laughter and jovial mood quickly became pinched and drawn as though a blanket laden with dung was thrown on them.

The old man was closing fast on Monty's mule, but as he started to pass, Monty reached over and whipped the other mule in the face. Undaunted, the mule surged forward, and the two raced ahead, neck and neck. Side by side, knee to knee, the old man knew that he and his mule were about to beat the boasting Monty Roberts. That's when Monty hit the man. With force and with conviction of his right to win, Monty Roberts swung with all his might at an old man having a good time. The fun was over. A photographer captured the moment. Los Rancheros Vistadores vowed silence to protect, but they asked Monty Roberts not to return.

Quarter horse breeders Greg and Mary Whalen sent a horse to Monty for training. The stallion showed great potential as a performance horse. He might have been a champion. A good mover, the horse was light and responsive. If Monty could put a spin on him, he'd do well on the performance circuit. Monty assured his friends that he could do it.

Interview with Mary Whalen, Quarter Horse breeder, 1999:
"We don't know what happened to the horse when he was with Monty, but he came home with his neck and shoulder area raw and swollen. The hair eventually grew back: dark, dark hair on a very light gray stallion."

Interview with Mindy Waltrip Tidwell, Neighbor and student, 1998:

"I was four years old when Marguerite and Marvin moved next door to our family on River Road.

"It didn't take long for me to become Marvin's shadow, following him around whenever I could. In time, he taught me to groom, to ride, to respect, and to care for horses. He always let me ride whatever extra horse might be available. I loved the horses from the minute I first saw them.

"For more than sixteen years of my life, I saw Marvin and Marguerite almost daily. I was shocked to learn of Monty's allegations regarding his parents. I certainly never saw Marvin be cruel to a horse or a human. I do remember being amazed that he could actually ride a horse without a bridle.

"He used to tell me that if I could become 'one' with my horse, I wouldn't need a bridle either. He had tremendous patience and taught me to respond to a horse with my body. He would tell me to pay attention to my horse and to respect what the horse was feeling. He taught me to watch my horse's ears and not to be afraid.

"My parents knew they could trust Marvin and Marguerite to make sure that I was safe. Marvin loved all of us. The horses loved him too. I never saw a mean bone in that man's body.

"I feel very fortunate to have had Marvin

Roberts lay the foundation of my horsemanship knowledge and skill. He taught me to be sensitive to my horse and to never be cruel.

"Marvin and Marguerite were like parents to me and to many others. They were the nicest people I have ever known. I have never met anyone like them. I didn't own a horse, and I wasn't a paying customer, yet they never once turned me away.

This new generation of riders did not personally know Monty well. They knew Marvin and Marguerite.

Marvin Roberts and Debbie Twist in 1979. (Salinas Californian. Clay Peterson Photo).

Some met Monty on the few occasions he ventured to Salinas. But all of them knew of his accomplishments and his success in the thoroughbred industry and his highly acclaimed Flag Is Up Farms in Solvang.

They knew because Marvin and Marguerite bragged about him. They were proud of him. Monty and Pat were part of the thoroughbred jet set, flying across continents and oceans as they bought, sold, and raced horses.

Interview with Marguerite Martins Happy, Monty's cousin, and Roberts student, 1997:

"Uncle Marvin unselfishly and without payment helped me a great deal when I ran for Hostess at the California Rodeo in Salinas. He also hired my boyfriend, Clifford Happy, to ride colts for him.

"He taught Cliff a lot about breaking colts, and during the time Cliff worked for him there was never any cruelty served to the colts. After Cliff and I were married, we bought Johnny Twist from Uncle Marvin. He was by Monty's stud, Johnny Tivio.

"Uncle Marvin knew I wanted to make a barrel racing horse out of Johnny Twist. He was quite stern with his advice. He told me that a lot of barrel racers run their horses over and over but that was not wise. He said I should do a lot of slow work and not whip my horse to get him to work for me. I should score him a lot in front of the barrel pattern and make sure my horse stayed calm before I ran."

"Marvin Roberts was the grandfather I never had. For nearly twenty years, his picture has been on display in my home. He taught me not only the ways of horses, but also the ways of cowboys. He changed my life.

"For ten years I listened to his words of judgment on dozens of horses and yet never heard him render even one word of judgment on a person. His cowboy psychology, zest for life, and simple, joyous nature carried me through many rough times. With Marvin, I felt safe.

"I met Marvin and his horses at a time when my days were often bleak. It was the summer of nineteen seventy-five. I had left a broken marriage in another state and was fighting depression when I decided to pursue my childhood dream of learning to ride.

"I opened the yellow pages, found a name, a telephone number, and met a horseman named Marvin Roberts.

"From Marvin I learned early to do the right thing around a horse so that I would not be physically injured nor would my horse be harmed. To this day, I consider myself fortunate to have known and learned from him. He concerned himself with my physical safety at the stable, but gave me emotional security as well.

"My hours at [the Buena Vista Stables] were far more therapeutic than any antidepressant pill. Marvin had a way of making me feel

accepted and valued. Never once did I see him mistreat a horse nor a human.

"One busy Sunday there, I witnessed the owner of a young thoroughbred attempt repeatedly, without success, to lift the animal's hind leg, presumably to clean the hoof. Failing to get the desired response, the owner asked for help.

"Marvin immediately detached himself from the center of activity and went to assist. With a soothing touch and voice to match, Marvin proceeded to pick up the horse's foot in one fluid motion, seemingly without effort and with apparent full cooperation from the horse. To me, it was a great demonstration of horse handling and of understatement on Marvin's part. Never did he chastise or lecture the owner. He merely helped as needed. His actions taught the lesson."

Chapter 14

HORSE TRAINING PRINCIPLES

Marvin believed in certain core training principles that have proven valid over time. One is that a fearful horse can be dangerous to a human. Marvin believed a horse should be sacked out to help him overcome fear.

The Man Who Listens to Horses:

> Horses understood one thing only, my father barked, and that was fear. If you did not hurt them first, they would hurt you. (p.11)

> [My father] threw the sack over the horses' backs and around their legs . . . . the horses panicked. They rolled their eyes and kicked, reared, and pulled back against the ropes as though their lives depended on it. . . . What primordial fears of attacks by predators were provoked? (p.39)

To repeat for clarity, *sacking out* is the term applied to a process that involves tossing a light canvas or plastic sack toward a horse, eventually touching his legs and body with the sack. In this way, the horse learns that not all objects coming toward him are predators. He also learns that strange sounds are not always harmful and do not necessarily mean pending death from which to flee for life.

It is through this sacking-out process that a horse learns to accept surprise. Here he learns that the human is not trying to hurt him. Imagine the strength of a one thousand pound domesticated animal who instinctively retreats when afraid or sensing danger. Even a seasoned veteran can flinch when the unexpected happens.

Suppose the cat, curled up on a bale of straw, spies a mouse and leaps in front of the horse as she chases her prey. Or perhaps the wind sends a hat, parka, or piece of paper sailing through the air. Any of these, or a dozen other situations, could cause a horse to shy, or bolt, or run, or rear back and paw the air to fend off the perceived attack. The key to success is preparation.

Crystal is sixteen now. She is the daughter of Cheri (Renebome) and Barney Little. Born just two years before Marvin and Marguerite died, she never had the opportunity to know them. But Crystal, perhaps more than any other person who has contributed to this book, provides an excellent example of the importance of Marvin's theories.

Marvin's goal was always a kind and disciplined horse that respected humans. His aim was a horse that could be trusted, would perform as requested, would be a joy to ride and a pleasure to be around. He also believed those lessons could be taught with kindness and that there was no need to be rough or abusive to any animal.

Interview with Crystal Little, Roberts grand niece and daughter of Barney & Cheri Little, 1998:

"It was a warm day on July seventh, nineteen ninety-three. I was ten and had been showing and riding horses my entire life. I had just gotten back from a show a few days earlier, where I rode my gelding Midnight Cocktail. I had done extremely well and my mom, Cheri Little, and I decided to give M. C. [Midnight Cocktail] the week off.

270

"I had a 4-H riding meeting to attend, and we decided to take my mom's new three-year-old colt, Tee Dee, for me to ride. I didn't want to miss this meeting because there was a trainer coming to help us prepare for the fair. My mom had never had a problem with Tee Dee I never imagined in my wildest dreams that making the decision to get on this young horse would change my life forever.

"When we arrived at the arena just outside of Longmont, Colorado, everything seemed relaxed. Everyone was in a good mood as we visited and tacked up our horses. Our leader, Jodi Zier, and all the parents were sitting in lawn chairs outside the arena chatting with the guest trainer.

"About five minutes before the trainer was going to start the lesson, I climbed on TeeDee and walked him to the arena. Usually my mom rode the horses before I got on, to be sure the playfulness was out of them, and they were ready for me to handle. However, she couldn't do that this night because 4-H rules state that the child must do their own project. A horse can not be ridden or trained by anyone but the child. As I got on, there was no doubt in my mind that this horse was safe for me to ride. He was very gentle for being only three.

"My mom walked me to the arena and made sure that I was going to be fine before she turned and joined the conversation of bystanders. As Tee Dee and I walked down the rail, a noise came

from the far end of the arena. Tee Dee's head jolted up in curiosity.

"I was beginning to think that maybe this wasn't such a good idea. I turned to head back to the gate—and my mother. As soon as I turned him around, Tee Dee seemed more afraid of the noise and began to run and crow-hop across the arena. I remember yelling for my mom.

"I heard Mom screaming for someone to shut the gate so that he didn't run out with me on him. Mom was yelling frantically for me to grab the reins to stop him as she ran towards me. It all seemed like slow motion, thinking about it now, but when it was happening there wasn't enough time for me to stop him. The next thing I remember was heading toward a huge iron fence.

"Tee Dee came to a jolting halt. I remember trying to maintain balance, but I bounced off his rump backwards, into the dirt. That is the last thing I remember before waking up surrounded by people. Mom told me that after Tee Dee ran into the fence and I fell off, he began to back up.

"As Tee Dee backed towards me I tried to roll over to get out of the way of this twelve-hundred pound animal. Before I could move, his foot slid across my face and chest, leaving a raw and bloody trail in the path of his aluminum shoe.

"As I came back to reality, I heard my mom yelling for Kelly Martinez to call an ambulance. My jaw felt really tight as I tried to tell my mom that I was fine. I began to try to stand up, but my mom guided me to lay back down. I actually thought I was fine until I saw that my mom and my friends that were trying to help me were all covered with blood—my blood.

"The guest trainer that would have given us our riding lessons comforted me as she asked me to move my toes and fingers to make sure that I didn't have a broken neck. No one knew exactly what was broken. By that time, an excruciating pain had set in, and I knew I did not want to die.

"When I was put into the ambulance, reality started to sink in. I hit the panic button when I overheard the medics telling my obviously upset mom the details of my injuries. A series of questions came out of my mouth.

"'Am I going to die?' 'Am I okay?' 'What happened?'

"As I was wheeled into the emergency room, I remember seeing the faces of friends and the girls that became known as my big sisters. The scared looks on their faces made me afraid and sick to my stomach.

"As the nurses were cleaning off my face, I became extremely upset with them. They were hurting me, and I was too young to appreciate that they were only trying to help me. They wiped my face with gauze and inserted an IV tube in my hand. My mom and some of my friends were allowed to come in and see me. They held my hand and told me that it would be all right. That helped me a lot. But that is when I began to wonder, 'Why?'

"I couldn't understand how a horse could do this to me. It just didn't seem fair.

"From the emergency room, I was taken to x-ray, which was not a pleasant experience for me. I cried through the whole thing because they made me sit up in a chair and by this time I was extremely weak. They discovered that I had a broken jaw, and I had to have a CAT scan. I was terrified as they put me into this big machine. I just wanted to turn back time so that I would never have gotten on that horse.

"Everyone felt helpless and upset, including my mom. She was blaming herself for putting me on a young horse. However, it was my wish to ride Tee Dee that day, and she never had reason to think that he wouldn't be safe for me.

"During the whole emergency room ordeal, our good friend Karen Turner tried to locate my dad, who was on a business trip in Idaho. I wanted to see my dad.

"From the CAT scan, I was next prepped for

Crystal Little and Midnight Cocktail at the world show in 1995. Cheri Little, Candy Owen, and Lee Metzger are also pictured.

surgery. I can remember being rolled down the hall to the surgery room like it was yesterday. I can still recall exactly what the ceiling looked like. My mom was back in the waiting room. We both knew I was in good hands. The doctors were nice. They explained most of what they were going to do before they did it.

"They basically would have to sew the bottom of my face back on. My jaw would have to be put back together with a metal plate, since I had barely any teeth left to wire it to. They would also have to sew my lower lip, which was like ground hamburger, back together.

"The last thing I remember before dozing off was the doctor shoving two plastic tubes up my nose. I asked him if he was trying to kill me. I was in surgery most of the night. My mouth required over seventy stitches to repair. I lost four permanent teeth, including my front three, and six baby teeth.

"When I woke up after surgery, my mom was standing over me with a big smile on her face. She told me that the doctor had done a great job of sewing me up and that my dad was on his way.

"Over the next few days, many tears were shed and many people came to visit me. Their prayers and thoughts were greatly appreciated. I was in the hospital for five days (one of which was my mom's birthday). When I got home, I kept breaking out in tears. I was so angry! I could not understand why this had to happen to me! What *had I done to deserve this? I was most upset because I had to have fake teeth and live with scars on my face for the rest of my life.*

"The road to recovery has been long and bumpy. With the support of my mom and dad, I was back on a horse in three weeks. I was very nervous my first time back on. My dad was right by my side holding my hand. I felt like I had to ride again not just to make my parents happy, but to prove to myself that I could do it.

"I showed at my county fair August ninth, one month after my accident. I went to that fair toothless and frightened, but with the help of my loving parents, my friends, and my wonderful 4-H leader, Jodi Zier, I walked away a grand champion.

"I am now sixteen and continue to show and ride regularly. I [qualified and] showed at the American Junior Quarter Horse World Championship Show on Midnight Cocktail, and that was a dream come true, a goal I attained.

"I now have a partial retainer with my three front teeth on it. I have practically lived at the dentist's office for the past five years but have learned to accept reality. My scars continue to fade. They don't even bother me that much any more.

"The accident changed the way I think and ride. I never relax on my horses. I'm not sure I will ever be able to trust a horse one-hundred percent. Whenever a horse jerks his head at a

noise, my heart skips a beat as I remember that warm day in July."

Crystal continues to show horses and is a top competitor at local, state, and national shows.

After the accident, Cheri put Tee Dee in training. He overcame his fears, became a great youth horse, and won many 4-H championships. Ironically, the Little's sold Tee Dee to the dentist who treated Crystal.

Follow a Dream

Interview with Cheri Renebome Little, Joyce's daughter and Roberts student, 1997:

"Marvin Roberts was and will always be my hero. He is my guardian angel. Every day I ride, and every day he is with me. Whenever I get to having trouble with a colt, I always stop and think, 'How would Uncle Marvin do it?'

"He was a master horseman. One of the last great California reinsmen who rode using a spade bit and started his horses in a hackamore. Marvin was a master with the hackamore. His horses were so light and responsive that one barely need to ask, with the lightest, gentlest touch, and his horses would stop and spin on a dime.

"Marvin and Marguerite Roberts taught me everything I know about basic horsemanship. To keep my heels down and chin up; to never, never jerk on a horse's mouth; how to saddle a horse, groom a horse, and tie a horseman's knot. They

taught me to clean my tack, to never put a hat on the bed, or [to] tuck my pants inside my boots. They gave me my first pair of chaps. But they gave me a greater gift, a gift that comes from the heart, a gift that cannot be put into words. Just being around them was pure joy. I look back now and realize how extremely fortunate I was to have these people in my life.

"As a young girl, I spent summers and weekends riding at the Buena Vista Stables on River Road. It was Uncle Marvin who usually played the role of baby-sitter to us. Aunt Marguerite was working then. She had taken a job in town to help make ends meet and worked in the children's department at J. C. Penneys. Later, she worked sorting culls in the carrot sheds of Salinas.

"My best friend at the stables was my second cousin, Lynn Roberts. Lynn was probably closer to Marvin and Marguerite in their last years than any other person.

"There are so many stories to tell of those days; looking back they are very precious memories to me. I never once remember Uncle Marvin getting mad at us, losing his temper with a horse or a child, or even being grumpy. He always had a smile on his face and was always telling us stories. Aunt Marguerite would come home from work and scold him for indulging us.

"Aunt Marguerite never let us get away with much. She was definitely the boss. I remember the time Lynn and I took our horses out and raced *through Massolo's cornfields. Oh, what a blast that was! Of course, we knew we weren't supposed to do it, but it was so much fun! I probably remember it so well because it was such a devilish thing to do, and we felt like hooligans.*

"Occasionally, Lynn and I would bring the horses back sweating and hot because we had been running them and having way too much fun. If Aunt Marguerite ever caught us doing that, there was hell to pay! Physically, she wouldn't hurt a fly, but she was bombastic with us if she thought we were doing anything that might harm the horses. She taught us well.

"Uncle Marvin would caution us quietly to make sure we always cooled the horses, which we did, but he had a way of making us feel guilty all the same. He seemed to understand that we enjoyed the excitement of a good run and probably the horses did too. He maintained enough of a somber attitude to remind us that we should always use caution."

Interview with Cheri Renebome Little regarding her apprenticeship with Marvin Roberts, 1998:

"I was sixteen and drove an old Ford truck and pulled a red Miley horse trailer. My rig wasn't fancy, but I bought it with money I earned from raising, showing, and selling steers at the Monterey, Salinas Valley, and Santa Cruz fairs. At the time, I had a bay mare called Momma.

"I started going out to Uncle Marvin's to get help with Momma's training. It didn't take long

to realize that *Uncle Marvin and Aunt Marguerite were in desperate need of help. It was obvious even to a girl of only sixteen.*

"Marguerite was working in those cold packing sheds. At fifty-six years old, she stood

Cheri Little riding Momma during Big Week, Salinas, 1974. (Photo courtesy of Cheri Little).

over a conveyor belt all day, sorting carrots bound for market or the cull trucks. I wanted to help. Uncle Marvin was already getting stiff in the joints, and it's hard to keep decent help around when you haven't got much to pay.

"I rode colts and did what I could. Looking back, I wish I'd done more. It was during this time that Uncle Marvin began to teach me the art of using a hackamore, working a colt on the lines, tying a leg up, sacking out, and his entire program. Monty calls Marvin's training methods cruel and says or implies that Marvin's horses obeyed out of fear. He paints an ugly picture of a man torturing horses to have them obey. This is a totally distorted view of the truth.

"All of Marvin's horses were taken through the same steps, and the end result was a horse that had respect for his handler and a horse that was safe to be around. A horse that, as Marvin would say, 'Learned to take his surprises.'"

Marvin Roberts made moments like this possible for Marguerite Happy and Jessie Reigh Evans.

Key Principles

Here then are a few of Marvin's key principles.[20]

The finished horse understood that he need not be afraid of people, or loud noises, or flying objects around the barn. The finished horse had manners. A person did not have to sneak around him. He stood while being mounted, and he turned, stopped, and backed when asked. This horse was soft in the mouth and could be ridden with a light hand on the rein. This horse knew and trusted people. This was a horse that could handle the unexpected without panic.

Marvin usually started colts when they were nearing three years of age. Their legs and knees were developed by then, and they were less prone to injury and leg problems.

His first step was to tie up a leg. He did this to teach a young horse to stand still while being groomed and handled. The horse was not hurt or punished by having a leg tied. The horse was simply restrained from moving around. Farriers particularly appreciate a horse that has learned to stand still.

To tie up a hind leg, Marvin used a very thick, very soft cotton rope with a leather cuff that went around the

---

[20] It should be stressed again that inclusion here does not mean this is the only way to train or cure bad habits, only that they worked for Marvin. His horses respected him and loved him. They worked willingly and were his partners. There are many wonderful trainers today who disagree with Marvin's methods of horse training. There are also many wonderful trainers who incorporate portions of Marvin's training principals with ideas and methodologies of their own or from others. The important issue is keep a good attitude, remain calm, and use the elements that work best for you and your horse. A gentle demeanor and sensitivity are always best. If you experience difficulties with your horse, it is always best to seek the advise of a professional horse trainer.

rear pastern. A bowline knot was tied around the neck and the cuff was sent down the line, and it was a neat little trick to wiggle it down the leg and finally around the pastern. He would then pull up the slack and gently raise the horse's hoof a few inches off the ground—just enough to keep him restrained. The end of the rope was tied off on the neck rope. A calm and soothing voice is used the entire time.

In this position, the horse is of no danger to the handler or in risk of imposing injury on himself. Most professional trainers do not consider this practice, when done correctly, to be abusive or cruel. It is a means of restraint. It is important to note that horses that are handled from a very young age rarely need to have this done.

> *[Lawrence Scanlan writes that the rope in a black and white photo in Marvin's book is "clearly stained with blood." Perhaps he sees black and white in color. A light colored rope could be stained by manure as easily as by blood.*
>
> *Monty asks readers to believe that his father tied the legs of colts until, ". . . the horses had blood tracks on their pasterns where the ropes had worn through the skin; in places, friction burned off the hair. Bruising and more serious leg injuries were common," wrote Monty. (p.40)*
>
> *This is absurd. There are hundreds of people who watched Marvin work with horses from the early 1930s until his death in 1985. Marvin never treated a horse in such a manner.]*

Once the colt is comfortable, he is sacked out.

Sacking out has come under a great deal of criticism. Monty calls this an abusive practice. Some trainers agree with him. Many other respected trainers disagree. You might remember from a previous chapter that this process involves the tossing of a lightweight sack around a colt, gradually working up to gently tossing it across and over his back and rump. Marvin liked to use plastic because it made a little noise. He would talk to the horse with a calm and soothing tone the entire time, assuring the horse that he had nothing to fear.

The colt soon trusted Marvin and would stand relaxed and unafraid, even if Marvin rattled the plastic. He understood there was no threat and that he would not be hurt. There are many signs to tell when the horse is relaxed and responsive—a lowering of the head; licking and chewing; the ears now watch, or move, with the sack. Following these exercises, a horse is usually safer to ride and be around. He is less likely to shy at unexpected surprises that might come his way.

Next came the first saddling. Marvin restrained the leg again to saddle the horse. The horse was *not* thrown to the ground. He was also introduced to the hackamore at this time. After the colt was confident with everything about being saddled, his leg was released, and he was reined up in the corral. Here he is able to walk around with the saddle and hackamore. The reins are tied to the saddle horn. The colt quickly learns to drop his chin and give to the pressure of the hackamore.

This giving to the hackamore is self-taught. The colt learns to find his own release from the pressure by dropping his chin and flexing at the poll, thus backing off the pressure. After the colt is soft and responsive in the hackamore, the line work begins. Two long lines are hooked to a small piece of leather that runs through the hackamore at the chin. The lines are run through the stirrups, and the handler stands in the center of the corral.

This appears similar to lunging, but whips are never used and the handler has full control over the animal's head just as if he were mounted. The colt is already responsive to the hackamore. He is worked at the trot, then at a lope. He is taught to travel both right and left, learning his leads during the process. He becomes comfortable and confident at performing under saddle and doing all that is asked of him.

Marvin's horses were well schooled before anyone ever sat on their backs. In all our years with Marvin, we don't remember one serious accident involving a person and a horse or Marvin ever being hurt by a horse. This was no coincidence. After the line work for several days, the colts were mounted without incident and training progressed from there.

Days Grow Short

The morning of October 9, 1983, promised the day would be one of those very special autumn days in the Salinas Valley. The morning air held a slight chill, but the sun was bright and the customary fog lay coiled like cotton candy over the Monterey Bay leaving Salinas to bask in the sunshine.

More than 175 friends and relatives made their way to the Monterey County Sheriff's Posse Grounds. It was hard to believe it had been nearly fifty years since their wedding day.

Marguerite's eyes misted as she spoke to her sister, it was a happy occasion, but she wished their oldest son could be there too. His business took him away she said.

The posse grounds were alive with well wishers. Decorated and festive, Marvin and Marguerite were nearly overwhelmed by the sea of faces that stopped to kiss, hug, and tell them how much they were loved. Marguerite's sister, Tiny, had spent weeks organizing and planning this wonderful party. She had wanted it to be a surprise, but knew it would be difficult to know whom to invite without their help.

On the table with the cake stood a beautiful money tree with instructions that the couple was to use the tree's fruit for a trip to Hawaii. All arrangements had been made and no argument would be accepted. The vacation was long, long overdue.

On the way home that night, Marguerite cried and shared with her son Larry that this day had made an entire life seem very worthwhile and Marvin agreed. Larry felt the blessed joy of having parents possessed of such incredible love for humankind and for each other. Always focused on others, they were rarely self-indulgent. He knew they were unique, special people and felt extreme pride and honor that they were his parents.

Surely, God holds a special place for them, Larry thought. *I wish Monty were here.*

As the years inexorably marched on, Marvin and Marguerite continued their vigilant watch over horses, children, and the river. Each new day brought simple joys, new aches, and more work. There was never an end to the work.

There were horses to be fed, stalls to clean, fences to mend, and alleys to rake. There was equipment to be repaired, lessons to give, horses to be trained, and children to be supervised. There was also a house to clean, laundry to be done, meals to prepare, and errands to run.

With limited financial resources, Marvin and Marguerite did not always have hired help available. They may have been doing the work they loved, but as they aged, it exacted a toll on the couple.

Marguerite and Larry.

"Marguerite cried and shared with her son Larry that this day had made an entire life seem very worthwhile and Marvin agreed."

Part IV

He Learned to Win

The Red Pony

    At the top of the ridge Jody was winded. He paused, puffing noisily. The blood pounded in his ears. Then he saw what he was looking for. Below, in one of the little clearings in the brush lay the red pony. In the distance, Jody could see the legs moving slowly and convulsively. And in a circle around him stood the buzzards, waiting for the moment of death they know so well.

—John Steinbeck

Chapter 15

THE END CAME TOO SOON

Their days and years were peppered with good times, good friends, and the satisfaction of giving. But as days and years do, they took a toll on Marvin and Marguerite. The last few years may have been the hardest. Marguerite tried to hide her pain, though her pain was genuine and it was great.

She was nearing seventy, though she was relatively certain she would not live to see that day. She spoke often of years gone by and would smile with the warmth of her memories. Perhaps they helped keep her warm as she worked to sort produce in the local packing sheds, ignoring the cold like she ignored the cancer making its way through her body.

Friends who stopped to visit usually encountered a rather stiff-in-the-joints and down-in-the-back Marvin doing his best to keep a stable full of the horses he loved for the students he doted on. In his mid-seventies, he wore glasses that made his eyes look three times larger than normal. He would give the perfunctory grin as he nodded and said, "Yeah, everything's fine here. Marguerite's at work. Oh, yes, she's fine. She'll be home in a few hours."

As tough as she was, for all that she gave to others, Marguerite rarely took for herself. She was the rock.

The cancer spread. It claimed victory over Marguerite on April 30, 1985. Marvin was devastated, lost in a world without her. His boys came home.

They wanted to take him somewhere, but Marvin was confused. He told them that they couldn't leave without her. He couldn't leave without Marguerite.

"She'll be there," they assured him. "Dad, she's waiting for us at the funeral home. This is her funeral."

"Yeah, okay," he said as he remembered where they were going.

"Where did everyone come from?" Marvin asked of no one in particular. So many people were there. There were people he hadn't seen in years.

It had been so long since they had all been together. Marguerite would like this, he said aloud. It seemed like the entire town of Salinas was there.

The most important human relationship Marvin had ever known was gone. His boys had lives of their own. They had flown safely from the nest but were as different as night day. She had always been there for him. She filled his cup when it was empty. She gave him hope when things looked black. She never quit and she never gave in. What was he going to do without her?

Monty recalled that only a few people attended his mother's funeral service because her life had been spent entirely in the service of her husband and her children.

The cancer took her life in a most indignant fashion. The lies that were published about her life, and the life of her husband, took her dignity.

Marvin Roberts died just forty-five days after Marguerite lost her battle with cancer. It was not so much that Marvin lost the will to live, but rather that he willed himself to die. That was his wish and his desire: to be with his love, his life, his Marguerite.

HORSEFEATHERS

If you look to the heavens on a star-filled night
You'll find two Diamonds that shine so bright.
You'll see them surrounded by a hundred more
Twinkling stars with sparkle galore.

When the Lord took Marvin and his Marguerite, dear,
He knew they'd need children to teach and be near.
He gathered the wee ones that were taken too soon,
And a hundred white horses for a ride to the moon.

He took them to Marvin and said, "My good man,
Will you and your loved one teach what you can?
There are none better suited to handle this chore.
No others came close to matching your score."

Now for all you that wonder if horses can fly,
Just gaze in the dark at the stars in the sky.
If the night is quite still and free from all sound,
You may hear the echo, "Chin up, heels down."

And if you believe, you might glimpse a sight,
Of a hundred young riders on steeds in full flight.
Led by two Legends on horses pure white,
With soft feathered wings that glow in the night.

—Joyce Martins Renebome

Testimonial from Betty Dolan Kent, Family friend, 1998:

"In all the years that I was around the Roberts, I never saw Marvin strike either of his boys, let alone beat either one. If anything, Marguerite was the disciplinarian. When the boys became too rowdy, Marvin might step in and send one to his room and the other would remain in the dining room.

"Jack and I have not read Monty's book. The lives of the Roberts and the Martins were open books. They all loved to talk and share. When something happened to a member of the family, bad or good, everyone knew it immediately. Theirs was not a family that kept secrets."

Testimonial from Dee Dee Garcia White, Roberts student, 1998:

"All the years that I spent around Marvin Roberts, I never saw him mistreat anyone. Marguerite was always the disciplinarian in the family. Marvin spoiled us, and we loved it.

"Monty also talks about Nola Hightower, a Black woman who worked for the Roberts and for us. He says that Marvin was nice to her, but offensive behind her back because she was Black.

"Nola was never thought of as anything but family. The color of her skin didn't matter. She worked for both of our families for many years and still visits every week."

Testimonial from Joyce Martins Renebome, 1997:

"Marvin and Marguerite taught far more than basic riding skills. They taught students to be one with the horse. They continued their importance in my life, passing their vast knowledge to our children, who all love horses.

"In their later years, when they were struggling financially, Marguerite was forced to work in the packing sheds to make ends meet. In spite of their limited financial resources, I remember that they had two beautiful hand-tooled Western saddles custom made for their granddaughters.

"I remember wondering if Monty appreciated his wonderful parents. I now have the answer."

Testimonial from Carol Ann Roberts Silva, Marvin's niece, Ray Roberts daughter, 1998:

"My beautiful memories of my uncle and aunt, will not be changed by Monty.

"Marvin was a great person. He was a gentle giant of a man and reminded me of John Wayne sitting in the saddle. Monty talks in his book about his championship awards, but he overlooks the biggest award of his life—two parents that loved him and gave him and his brother everything they possibly could.

"Marvin and Marguerite did a lot for the kids in the Salinas Valley. If anyone wants the truth about my aunt and uncle, they need to come to Salinas. If they ask the ranchers in the area or

*people on the street that knew them, they will
learn the truth.*

*"My twin sister and I were lucky enough to be
included [with the other students] for riding
lessons. No matter what mistakes we made, I
never once remember him yelling at us. He would
explain the consequences of various mistakes so
that no accidents occurred around the horses.*

*"My father[Ray] and Marvin would give the
shirts off their backs to help others. I know that
neither had a prejudiced bone in his body.*

*"My parents mean the world to me. It broke
my heart when my mom died in November of
nineteen seventy-three from cancer. My dad was
diagnosed with melanoma cancer this year. He's
doing pretty good now, but is still sick. Our
parents were the best any kid could wish for. We
were never short on love in our home. My father
is the world to me and I know my twin sister and
both of my brothers feel the same."*

**Testimonial from Roy & Andrée Forzani, Professional horse trainers,
1998:**

*"Roy and I are just two of the many people
who consider Monty Roberts book and the articles
we've read about him to be preposterous trash
for the most part. They are unjust and
inflammatory, especially to his immediate family
members. His exploitation of the dead is
disgusting."*

Testimonial from Angie Garcia, friend, 1998:

"Monty still has my rolltop desk. I loaned it to Marguerite years ago. After she and Marvin both died so close together, I called Monty to arrange to get my desk back. He asked if I had any proof that it was mine, and I told him that I didn't, but that I'd loaned it to his mother years and years ago. He told me that all of her things went to him, and he would not let me have my own desk back!

"I can't prove that he didn't go around to horse shows in a boxcar either, but he didn't.

"It's sad to say, but I'm glad that Marvin and Marguerite are already buried in peace. If they were alive and knew what Monty is saying about them, it would likely kill them."

Testimonial from LaVonne Holt Kelley, Marguerite's niece, 1998:

"For someone who was incarcerated for allegedly conning people, it is hard to understand why so many people give Monty's story credence or why no one wants to know the true lack of character that he represents.

"Other people in Salinas and friends have sent me articles about Monty. I now feel the need to say that he is not a relative of mine. I hope that this collection of memories will celebrate the lives of two giving and dedicated individuals, Marvin and Marguerite. They richly deserve to be lauded for the way that their friends and family remember them.

"I live in an area not far from Monty. In all the years that I have lived here, I have not heard

much good about him or his dealings in the horse business. He is generally not trusted nor respected by his neighbors.

"In all the time that I was growing up, I never heard anything about Monty except how he won all kinds of ribbons, trophies, buckles, etcetera, at horse shows. I have a photo album that my mother kept of newspaper clippings of the shows he and Larry won. Monty seemed to accept all this as his right. He always acted like he was better than everyone, including his parents.

"My mother told me that she was with Marguerite and Marvin in town one day, and Monty would not acknowledge his own parents. My mother told me it was not the first time he had done such a thing. Yet I believe he says it was the other way around in his book.

"My memories of Marvin and Marguerite remain untarnished. Never would I believe the slander that their son is spewing to the world. It is sad to know what a classless, unsatisfied person Monty Roberts truly is. My professional opinion, holding a master's degree in counseling and guidance, is that Monty needs to seek help in resolving unfinished business in his life. A quiet consultation without media involvement is recommended."

Testimonial from Mindy Waltrip Tidwell, neighbor and student, 1998:

"Marvin's daily words and actions are directly opposed to the claims of his oldest son,

298

Monty. It doesn't make sense. I have an extremely difficult time understanding how Monty could claim that his father was cruel and his mother was meek. Those are definitely not the Marvin and Marguerite that I knew for sixteen years.

"I traveled to Solvang, and to Monty and Pat's Flag Is Up Farms, after Marvin's death. I did hope to have a last visit with Marvin's beloved mare, Debbie Twist. I was sure Monty took her after Marvin passed away but no one was around that knew anything about her."

Testimonial from Marguerite Martins Happy, Marvin and Marguerite's niece and student, 1998:

"Monty's book [British version] was given to me as a gift. [At the beginning] I was thinking, wow, what an interesting life. Why hadn't Aunt Marguerite, Uncle Marvin, or anyone else in the family shared all these fascinating stories about Monty?'

"When I spoke to enough people about claims in the book, the seed of doubt I had after the Dateline *show disappeared. A man that can make so many false stories about his life can surely lie about his father. Uncle Marvin and Aunt Marguerite are deceased and cannot stick up for themselves, so I believe out of respect and admiration we must speak up for them.*

"We have received so many calls and letters from old friends that it is unbelievable. We have not found one person that remembers things as

Monty does. People have in fact called in dispute of this so-called autobiography.

"I am writing this after receiving a family letter from Monty in December of nineteen ninety-six. His letter to many members of our family was in answer to many criticizing articles the family had written in an attempt to make the public aware that a number of people have different recollections of Monty's life. In Monty's family letter he stated that, 'It hurts that certain members of the family would choose to do this without investigating the full story first.'

"I decided to be fair and investigate as best that I could. What I have uncovered is that so much of what Monty says happened in his life is untrue, how then am I to believe the nasty things he says about his father?

"When you pick up a nonfiction book to read, you expect it to be fact, not fiction. In this case, however, I do not believe most of what is written in The Man Who Listens to Horses to be true. There is not one person I know who believes much of Monty's book.

"I have seen Monty's talent, and it is exceptional. He is nationally renowned and has worked hard to get where he is today. Nevertheless, it breaks my heart that he has allowed so many untrue happenings to be released in his autobiography.

"Where he is headed tomorrow is another story. Only Monty lives with his conscience. I definitely agree with Monty on one point, 'I will *accept criticisms where criticisms are due and even for differences of opinion, but outright untruths are not acceptable.'"*

Testimonial from Jane M. Harry, Roberts student, 1998:

"Among Monty's statements and innuendoes that his father trained with cruelty and dominance, I recognized a photograph of Marvin shown with a horse that is tied up and lying on the ground. It is from Marvin's own, Horse and Horseman Training[21] *book. On page twenty-two, in reference to that picture, Marvin wrote, 'Sometimes it is necessary to lay a colt down for altering [castration], or a horse that may need attention when it is impossible to do so with him standing.'*

"I do not interpret this as a breaking of the spirit type of thing. As he explains the placement of the ropes, Marvin wrote, 'In this way the colt will sit down and roll over on his side without bumping his head or mouth on the ground.' This shows a concern for the animal that Monty seems to have completely overlooked.

"As he helped to heal my aching spirit those many years ago, Marvin's true spirit will now always be safe with me."

---

[21] Marvin E. Roberts, *Horse and Horseman Training*, (Salinas, CA 1957).

1998, A LETTER TO MONTY

As days lengthened to weeks and months, the question that plagued the family was, Why? Why had Monty done this to his parents' reputation?

After months of prayer, perhaps the best explanation came from Cheri Renebome Little. When she shared her theory, sense overrode chaos. Cheri outlined her theory and feelings in a personal letter to her cousin. On September 1, 1998, she wrote:

Dear Monty,

It's been two years since I first learned about *The Man Who Listens to Horses.* Since that first *Dateline NBC* airing, I started on an emotional roller coaster that took me back to my childhood, through my teenage years, and into the present. I listened, I read, I agonized, but mostly I prayed.

During the time your book was on the best-seller list, there was another book out titled *Talking to Heaven* by James VanPraugh. This book caught my eye. I saw the author on *Larry King Live* and decided to buy the book. I found it very interesting to say the least.

In his book, VanPraugh says that spirits [the dead] often try to contact living people using ordinary electrical currents and telephone lines, etc. This offered a possible explanation to some bizarre things going on in my home during this tumultuous period of our lives.

The television came on at odd hours in the middle of the night, the smoke detector blared for no apparent reason, and my daughter's stereo came on full blast when I was talking to you on the telephone. Especially eerie was the time I was writing a letter about you on the computer when the telephone rang. When I answered, there was only the sound of my own voice echoed back to me. The line was open, yet there was no person on the other end.

I started to wonder if Marvin and Marguerite's spirits were trying to tell me something. Agonized and tormented, I prayed for answers. Monty, this may sound crazy to you, but I believe your parents really *were* trying to tell me something. I prayed to God for guidance.

I received my answer two nights ago. I was in bed and had just finished my prayers when a strange thing happened. I was suddenly filled with an overwhelming sense of love and peace, and I knew that I finally had my answer from God. I then drifted into a very peaceful sleep.

The next morning, I wrote this outline:

- *Monty grew up learning to be competitive.*
- *Monty found he liked to win.*
- *Later, Monty became determined to win.*
- *Ultimately, to Monty, winning is everything.*

The words continued to flow from my pen:

Monty saw himself as better than everyone around him, but there was one person he could not best. There was one person he could not get around or out from under. That was Marvin. No matter what Monty did as an adult in the horse world, to those that knew, the credit ultimately shifted to Marvin, the father, the Master Horseman.

303

When Queen Elizabeth II endorsed Monty, it seems that something must have snapped. Monty appears to have been awestruck. But it also seems that he had one final hand to play.

Monty apparently then set out to destroy the one obstacle he could never get around: the reputation of his father, Marvin Roberts. There was no room for sharing the glory. It was to be all Monty.

Monty, God is your judge, and He will judge you. I believe in the power of prayer, and I believe good wins over evil, all in a matter of time. You blew it with me when you lied to me about the *Ropers Sports News* article, the hateful things you said to me about Marvin on the phone, and the way you twisted the words from Marvin's book to make it look like he started his horses by beating them.

In the large scheme of things, your thirty-minute dance with a horse in a round pen is a lot of smoke and mirrors next to the lifetime of teaching horses and people that Marvin did. You could never fill his boots, could you Monty? Even if you have started ten thousand horses, sold your book to millions of people, donated money to charity, and brought an awareness to the public that horses can be easily taught if we only listen to them; you did so at an expense that was far too great. And you must live with that for the rest of your life.

Monty, I believe strongly in God. I do not hate you, but I do hate your lies and all you have put this family through. You know the truth, Monty. Deep in whatever soul you have left, Monty, you know.

The twenty years I rode and used Marvin's [horse training] methods I was never hurt or bucked off. Every show horse I get that hasn't been properly started has a [flaw] in it. They all need to be started over.

My daughter was almost killed in 1993 when a horse she was riding turned to flee from something that scared him. He ran into a fence, knocking her under it. He then proceeded to step on her face. He broke her jaw, Monty.

It took over seventy stitches inside and out to put her back together again. To this day, I know that horse should have been sacked out so it would not have feared the unknown. In all my years with Marvin, I was not hurt, and I don't remember any wrecks. Can you say that about your training program? I know that you can't.

I believe, Monty, that you are going to continue to get people hurt. Marvin was right, and you know it. Horses *can* hurt people. They do not need to be trained with dominance and cruelty. Your father didn't train that way, and you know it. I don't train that way, and most reputable trainers aren't cruel either. It's an ugly allegation for you to insinuate that they do.

One more thing: If you never had one day of admiration in your life for your father—and you supposedly say that you only learned what *not* to do from him—then would you please do away with the line work in your act? That, Monty, is how your father trained, only using the hackamore; otherwise it is the same—100%. You might also look over chapter 11, page 57, in his book. There he offers a method to teach a horse to catch that looks very much to me like an unpolished version of your Join-Up.

Please don't bother to write me again. I needed to get this off my chest, and it's the last you will hear from me. I believe your only hope for salvation is to ask God for forgiveness. I hope that you do.

I am not your judge, but from everything I see, your soul has been sold to the devil, and you have eternal damnation to look forward to after a life of being admired here on earth.

Maybe, just maybe, the publication of *Horse Whispers & Lies* will cause you to reflect on your giant sins, and you will seek forgiveness from whatever God you now worship. If you do, I will be happy for your soul, and I know your parents will be eternally grateful that our actions saved you from this path to hell you are so desperately trying to follow.

—Cheri Renebome Little

A Special Touch and Cheri Little in 1994.

Chapter 16

Phraseology

In 1957, Marvin called it Training a Horse to Catch.

In 1997, Monty calls it Join-Up. Monty's Herculean effort to promote himself, his book, and a nonviolent method of horse training has generally been well received across this continent and abroad. Many of his clinics' attendees are mesmerized by Monty's almost mystical power over the horse. How does he do it?

In the 1960s, Dr. William "Billy" Linfoot, a veterinarian from Pleasanton, California, offered demonstration clinics on a method of working with horses that would allow him to mount a "wild, unridden" horse in a matter of minutes. He used the terms "Advance and Retreat" and "Approach at a forty-five degree angle." A review of Dr. Linfoot's early films offers a glimpse of the natural horsemanship wave to hit the horse industry. Marvin Roberts was a fan of Dr. Linfoot and often spoke highly of the equine veterinarian.

In *Horse and Horseman Training*, Marvin E. Roberts offered advice on how to teach a horse to be caught in an open area. His directions were simple in 1957. He gave no reason for the action. He only offered that it worked.

- Use a corral about fifty feet in diameter, turn the horse loose.

- Take a rope about thirty-five feet long, toss it at the horse, and pull it back.

- Make him go one way around the corral and then the other.

- When he slows, make him go on, but do not whip him.

- Keep throwing the rope over his back or behind him.

- When he begins to tire, step in front of him, hands up, and say, "Whoa."

- If he stops, walk up and pet him.

- If he runs away, throw the rope over him and make him continue the run.

- Do this two or three times; soon he will face you when you walk toward him.

[22] Marvin E. Roberts, *Horse and Horseman Training,* (Salinas, CA 1957).

- Use a pen that is fifty feet in diameter.

- Have a light sash thirty feet long.

- Pitch the line toward his rear quarters, it will not hurt him.

- Keep the horse moving. He is retreating. You must advance.

- Get the horse to canter five or six revolutions one way.

- Reverse and repeat.

- When he wants to stop, coil the sash and assume a submissive mode.

- If he stands and faces you, move closer to him, but not straight on.

- Soon he will reach out with his nose to your shoulder, this is Join-Up.

Marvin called it Line work.
Monty calls it Line work.

Marvin believed that line work was another step in teaching a horse. He believed that with line work a horse could learn manners, get the feel of the hackamore, and learn to stop, turn, and change leads before he was ever ridden.

[23] Monty Roberts, *The Man Who Listens to Horses,* (New York, 1997).

- Use a buckskin string to form a loop at the knot of a rawhide hackamore.

- Attach the lines to top of the loop and run through stirrups on either side.

- Leave plenty of slack in the reins and attach them to the saddle.

- Put the colt between the lines.

- Get him to canter going either way.

- Stand in the center and let the colt go around you.

- Do not use a whip.

- Do not work him too long.

- If he stops, turn him away from you, do not use the line as a whip.

- Let the colt go the way he starts until he gets the idea.

- Then turn him toward the fence to go the other way.

- With race colts let them make large turns.

[24] Marvin E. Roberts, *Horse and Horseman Training*, (Salinas, CA 1957).

- Attach the lines to either side of the bit rings.

- Run the lines through the stirrups.

- Position the colt between the two lines.

- If inexperienced, try it with an older horse or you could hurt your horse or yourself.

- Ask your horse to circle at the canter and then trot both ways.

- Ask him to negotiate turns and stops.

- Finally, ask him to rein back one step.

- At this point, most horses are ready to be ridden, states Monty.

Indefatigable Promotion

Monty has done much to inform neophyte horsepersons that humans can and do communicate with horses in ways far removed from those seen in old Western movies. For this, he deserves applause. He has heightened awareness of the unique bond that can form between horses and humans. He is indefatigable as he works to deliver his message throughout the world.

Is this message new to horsepersons? Is this method of communication truly revolutionary? Or perhaps only refined over the last few generations? Is it possible that only the promotion of this methodology is revolutionary?

If Monty's how-to descriptions of Join-Up and Line Work appear similar to those employed by his father, or

---

[25] Monty Roberts, *The Man Who Listens to Horses,* (New York, 1997).

even Dr. Linfoot, could they also be similar to those of other respected horsepersons?

Natural horsemanship advocates in the United States recognize the names of Tom Dorrance, Ray Hunt, John Lyons, Pat Parelli, and Buck Brannaman. These clinicians, like Monty, are among those working to deliver the message. It's a good message.

According to one of Monty's colleagues, who asked not to be mentioned by name, it was in the 1970s that Monty Roberts attended one of Ray Hunt's horse training clinics in San Luis Obispo. Monty had by then worked extensively with thoroughbred racehorses and had made many trips to Europe. Watching Hunt, Monty suggested to his colleague and friend that if Hunt would trade his cowboy garb for British tweed and take his act to Europe, he'd really have something.

From demonstrations at various horse stables and at his own Flag Is Up Farms, Monty's book catapulted him to stardom. Riding his wave of notoriety, an idea germinated for a film about Monty and mustangs. The project was proposed to and accepted by the British Broadcasting Company, and plans were soon underway to film Monty as he joined up with a wild horse—actually in the wild.

Monty claimed that the documentary would allow him to do two things: he could say that he had done it before, and that he could still do it. This may have been important to him because the people who had been a major part of his life in 1952, when he claims to have previously joined up with a mustang in the wild, were already making statements that he had not.

For the project, Monty adopted three mustangs from the Bureau of Land Management (BLM) adoption program in 1996. He named one of them Shy Boy.

At the back of the United Kingdom paperback version of *The Man Who Listens to Horses,* Monty provides an explanation as to why he needed three wild horses.

The Man Who Listens to Horses, (U. K., paperback, 1998):

> I needed the back-ups because a number of things outside my control might go wrong. The mustang might run lame half-way through the shoot. He might be struck by a rattlesnake. . . . My three youngsters were run down the chute, unknowingly adopted for this unique project. (p.363)

> [Rattlesnakes] killed two horses [not mustangs] before the shoot even began. They strike at body heat and when they first emerge from their dark winter dens, they're cranky and unpredictable – a disaster waiting to happen. A struck mustang, and we might get by with our back-up number one or two. A saddle horse struck and it might be replaced. But myself struck – that would be the end of it. (pp.364, 365)

- **BLM Regulation #4770.1(e)** Forbids the commercial exploitation of wild horses or burros.

- **BLM Regulation #4700.0-5** Commercial exploitation means using a wild horse or burro because of its characteristics of wildness for direct or indirect financial gain.

- **BLM Regulation #4740.1(b)** Before using helicopters or motor vehicles in the management of wild horses and burros, the authorized officer shall conduct a public hearing in the area where such use is to be made.

Does the Bureau of Land Management not view Monty's use of Shy Boy as a commercial exploitation? Does the Bureau of Land Management believe that Shy Boy was treated in a humane manner after he was adopted by Monty?

Monty describes how Shy Boy was treated:

The Man Who Listens to Horses, (U. K., paperback, 1998):

I was driving the mustang, in full flight, over the high desert. . . . I hadn't reckoned on the level of panic caused by the helicopter [overhead]. In retrospect, I should have asked that it follow us only for the first 20 minutes and then back off, so we could have regrouped, read the situation as it developed.

Instead, the helicopter ran us to death. We covered nearly 100 miles in that first day, the mustang in full gallop for an hour and a half. It was an unforgettable ride. . . .

It was killing, to stay at a full gallop for an hour and a half, and a lot of the time I had to be up out of the saddle to spare the horses back. I was unsure of the ground and one stumble at that speed could have been fatal. . . . I practically ran my first horse, the Cadet, into the ground. He ended up with swollen legs but thankfully wasn't injured. (pp.366, 367)

- **BLM Regulation #4700.0-5(e)** Humane treatment means handling compatible with animal husbandry practices accepted in the veterinary community, without causing unnecessary stress or suffering to a wild horse or burro.

- **BLM Regulation #4750.3-2(3)(ii)** Until fence broken, adult horses shall be maintained in an enclosure at least six feet high: Materials shall be protrusion-free and shall not include large-mesh woven or barbed wire.

The Man Who Listens to Horses, (U. K., paperback, 1998):

And the fences were a horrible worry, as I'd predicted – but here the helicopter came into its own, overhauling the mustang and containing him. There were twelve miles between fences, but mustangs don't know barbed wire, they don't see it. . . . (p.367)

I made the decision to ride through the night on a horse called Big Red Fox. Big Red Fox was a Thoroughbred, retired . . . . It was a minefield of badger holes, but we didn't fall into any of those. (p.368)

Right at daybreak, around 4:30, [Shy Boy] took me on a high-speed chase for 15 miles. It was as harrowing as anything I'd ever ridden. There were no cameras, I'd been in the saddle for near enough 24 hours non-stop, but I kept on him. (p.369)

While Shy Boy may have been in excellent physical condition, several veterinarians, including one that works extensively with endurance race horses, have expressed the opinion that what Monty did to the mustang [as stated by Monty] was either unbelievable or unbelievably cruel, or both.

Monty, Shy Boy, and Big Red Fox were reunited to make a second video about a year after the one described above.

Judging from Monty's vivid description of the environmental conditions, it seems the inevitable finally happened.

1997–1998, BIG RED FOX

Monty's treatment of Big Red Fox was defined in a Superior Court complaint filed by Carolyn and Christopher Carradine on May 22, 1998. The twenty-seven-page document delineates alleged fraudulent and inhumane actions against the Carradine's gentle thoroughbred gelding by Monty Roberts and the British Broadcasting Corporation.

It seems that Monty used Big Red Fox in two documentary films that depict Monty as a horse communicator with the ability to gain a wild horse's trust without force or savageness. The suit contends that Monty rode Big Red Fox nonstop for over one hundred miles, causing the horse extraordinary fatigue. This ride, through a bitter cold night, caused trauma and injury to the horse's back, and he also became wet and was shivering with cold. The American Humane Association (AHA) was not contacted prior to making this documentary and did not have a representative on site during the shoot.

Later, while making a second video, the suit contends that Monty willfully turned Big Red Fox loose in the wilderness where he became lost just before dark. Much later that same night, Monty found the horse—with a broken leg. Worse still, Big Red Fox had cuts and bruises over two of his legs, and blood was pouring from numerous open wounds. A veterinarian on the set suggested that the battered horse would need no treatment.

316

Carradine was appalled. *(They were not yet aware the leg was broken).*

According to the complaint, Monty refused to take Big Red Fox to a veterinary clinic until morning. When he did, Carolyn informed Monty that she wanted to take her horse home. Monty became angry and enraged. The document reads: "He threatened Plaintiff Carolyn Carradine and stated 'This horse stays with me,' and 'I'll take you to the mat on this one.' . . . Roberts loaded up Big Red Fox in a trailer and drove away without informing [the owners] of what he intended to do for, or with, their injured, bleeding, cold and battered horse."

Monty took Big Red Fox back to the wilderness to use him to finish filming the second documentary that promotes Monty as a defender of animal rights and an advocate of kindness and nonconfrontational behavior.

Though the suit has been settled, the Carradines have not made the outcome public. According to a source who worked closely with Monty on the project, and who does not want to be named, Monty needed Big Red Fox on the second project because Big Red Fox had bonded with Shy Boy.

His own herd gone, Shy Boy formed a sort of friendship with Big Red Fox. In a sense, Big Red Fox had become Shy Boy's new herd. Without Big Red Fox along on the making of the second documentary, Shy Boy might not have returned to Monty at all. Or he might have. However, it doesn't appear that Monty was willing to risk failure. Big Red Fox was an insurance policy that Shy Boy would return.

Missy

When Monty travels around the country to promote Join-Up, where does he get the "wild," or "unhandled," horses that he uses in his demonstrations?

The telephone call came from a friend. Would Tina agree to allow a man named Monty Roberts to use her two-year-old half-Arabian colt for a demonstration in starting young horses that very evening?

The friend assured her this remarkable man could give her colt a good start, and Tina welcomed the prospect. This particular colt had been raised in the desert with little human contact and had only recently been brought in from the range. Tina was recuperating after a car wreck and faced a long recovery period. Her colt was a sure candidate if Monty wanted a horse that hadn't been handled much.

She agreed, and a pickup truck and a trailer soon pulled into her yard. Two men climbed out: a stocky fellow she assumed to be Monty Roberts and a younger man who turned out to be a locally hired assistant. Tina directed them to the corral where the colt was penned.

According to Tina, Roberts tried to get the colt's attention, then turned his back on the colt. He did this several times, but the colt showed no interest or willingness to come toward Monty. After a few minutes, Tina was told the colt could not be used but was given no explanation or reason.

Monty's attention was then drawn to a pretty Arabian filly. She was about the same age as the colt, but to anyone who knew horses, it was obvious she had been handled extensively. Her coat glistened, a testament to high maintenance and long hours of grooming. She moved toward the humans, eager for attention. Monty eyed her carefully then asked Tina if he could use this filly instead.

Surprised by the request, she responded immediately that it was out of the question. This horse, Missy, was her baby, her pet, her pride and joy. Tina had spent many hours working with Missy, though she had not yet ridden the filly. There was no way she wanted her baby to take part in some demonstration. Besides, she told Monty, the filly had never been taught to load in a trailer.

Using a combination of what Tina called charisma and intimidation, Monty got her permission to take the filly. Internally, Tina was uncomfortable that she had capitulated and disturbed that she felt she couldn't say "no" to him.

Hoping he would change his mind, she voiced concern about loading Missy in the trailer. Monty assured her it would not be a problem. He then had his assistant position the back of the trailer at the corral gate. With a rope behind Missy's rump, the two men physically coerced her into the trailer.

Tina stared in disbelief. In her opinion, this was not a gentle coaxing; this looked more like a strong arm kidnapping. She could not believe her eyes. Tina felt her filly was being traumatized, and it was her fault for saying yes.

When Missy finally entered the trailer, Monty closed the tailgate and jumped in the truck without further conversation. Tina watched her baby leave with the strangers.

Dazed that she had been manipulated so easily Tina stared after them. She was still staring when it happened. The truck lurched and stopped. The noise from the trailer was horrifying. The men got out and Tina hurried to see what had happened.

By the time she reached the rig, Monty had opened the tailgate and was taking Missy out of the trailer. Her head and chest were covered with blood. The filly had tried in desperation to escape through the small window.

Tina stared in shock at her beautiful filly who was shaking with fear. Monty handed Missy's lead to Tina. "She's no good to me now," was all that he offered.

Tina began to protest that Missy needed to see a veterinarian. Monty shrugged and said, "She'll be okay," as he got back in the truck. The two men drove away.

Tina's identity has been changed at her request.

Interview with "Tina", A horse owner, 1998:

"My vet later found that two of Missy's teeth had been knocked out. Accidents happen. But I did feel that Monty could have shown some common courtesy. He could have said, 'Thank you for your offer,' or, 'I'm sorry this happened.' He was in an all-fired-up hurry but he could have called later to see how she was doing."

1997, Cody

According to horse owners J Bartell and Ginger Marin, it started when they saw an advertisement in the *Los Angeles Times* promoting Monty Roberts' book and a live local demonstration. Their horse, Cody, was a mustang. Because Monty had spent time with mustangs, the idea of reading Monty's book and seeing him in person was particularly appealing. Impressed and excited by the Random House promotion, they ran out and bought the book along with tickets to the upcoming demonstration.

Bartell and Marin read *The Man Who Listens to Horses* with keen interest in hopes of learning more about how to communicate with Cody. They hoped to learn something from Monty's experience and expertise with mustangs, the same breed of horse they owned. They read tales of his trips to Nevada, the capturing and gentling of wild mustangs, and figured Monty could do for their horse what he supposedly had done for so many others.

After seeing Monty in person, they were even more enthralled with the charismatic trainer. Learning that Monty had an internet website, they bartered a training deal for their horse in exchange for a heavy ad campaign for Monty on their own website. The deal was struck with Monty's representative and son, Marty Roberts, who is a lawyer, with Monty's direct approval.

Cody was sent to Monty's farm where he remained for nearly six months. J and Ginger said they thought their horse was getting behavioral training. Yet shortly after Cody was returned to them, the mustang bolted for no apparent reason and trampled Ginger—nearly to death.

Disfigured for life, Ginger has not recovered emotionally or physically from the incident. J and Ginger had believed Cody incapable of such an act. They thought he had received behavioral training during the six months he was stabled at the Flag Is Up Farms with the legendary man who listens.

Shaken and wanting answers, J and Ginger said they reported the incident to Monty's son, Marty. When Marty admitted that Cody had not actually had *any* training, the couple confronted farm manager, Crawford

Hall, who confirmed that their horse had not been trained. Cody spent six months at the Flag Is Up Farms. His owners said they had provided thousands of dollars worth of internet service to the Roberts organization in the good faith exchange that Monty Roberts had listened to their horse and worked with him.

Had it all been a lie?

Monty Roberts himself finally called and admitted to the owners that he had neither seen nor touched their horse while it was at his facility.

It seems that Cody could have yelled. No one at the Flag Is Up Farms was listening.

J Bartell and Ginger Marin have filed a civil action against Monty Roberts on charges of fraud. The case is pending. Cody went to Southern California horse trainer, John Saint Ryan, who works with natural and gentle horse training methods. Saint Ryan and Cody's owners say that Cody is responding beautifully.

Marvin E. Roberts

Marvin Roberts believed that every horse should be given the opportunity to be a good horse.

Horse and Horseman Training, 1957:

Remember you cannot pull a horse hard in the bit and teach him anything without the chance of hurting his mouth or cutting his tongue.

A colt or horse can be schooled in the hackamore all his life. The age ruling comes from the show ring only.

The material in this book is the result of long and hard work with a lot of good trainers from the time I was a small boy. I have put many a colt into training. I am not setting it up to change the methods of any trainer; however, I do feel that there are pointers in this book that any trainer may benefit from. I believe this is the easiest and smoothest method and will come out with more good horses, fewer accidents, and one will enjoy the work he is doing and at the same time the colt will enjoy his part when he begins to work.

Just remember you cannot tell the colt what you want, and he cannot read. The only way to train a colt is to show him what you want him to do. A lot of colts are trained some things before they are ready and others have passed up steps they should have learned early in the game. Some steps are just never taught. Almost every colt will learn what you want if you just show him.

There is nothing more enjoyable than to train and ride a good working horse, or to watch a good working horse that you have trained. A poor grade of horse looks good if he works good, and the better looking horse looks bad if he will not work.

I would like to remind you that one or two works are not going to finish a colt. I suggest a colt be worked at least one hour a day and six days a week. It takes about six months to make a green working hackamore colt and up to a year for a good top working hackamore horse. It will take an additional year for a novice bridle horse, and the next year to finish him out.

A horse can go on learning each time you ride him if you will take a little time and show him a few times what you would like him to do. It is well to put the hackamore on him when starting him on some new lesson or to refresh his memory on others regardless of his age or working ability.

To Love & Honor

Nobel prize winning author John Steinbeck grew up in Salinas. His boyhood home is less than a block from Sacred Heart Elementary School, which Monty and Larry Roberts attended. On June 27, 1998, the National Steinbeck Center in historic Salinas celebrated its grand opening.

The 37,000-square-foot museum features exhibits depicting Steinbeck's life and literary works. Among the interactive and multisensory exhibits is the imaginative Red Pony Stall.

From the pages of Steinbeck's novelette about the relationship between a young boy, his father, and a red pony, the exhibit offers a hands-on approach to the responsibility and experience of horse ownership. It is designed with children in mind and epitomizes Marvin and Marguerite Roberts' teachings and legacy.

Thanks to the efforts of those who care, a dedication plaque is engraved: "Sponsored by the Friends and Family of Marvin and Marguerite Roberts."

Interview with Joanne Church Taylor Johnson, Spearhead of the National Steinbeck Center dedication, 1998:
"Marvin and Marguerite gave so much to the children of Salinas and hopefully, in time, [Monty] will be forgotten, but this memorial will live forever."

In time, the exhibit will include an interactive computer that will tell the story of Marvin and Marguerite Roberts and the legacy they left to hundreds of children in Salinas. Those children learned lessons at the stables far beyond how to ride a horse.

Interview with Mike McPharlin, Roberts riding student, 1998:

"From Marvin and Marguerite we learned horsemanship and how to grow up and behave as the next generation of adults for the town of Salinas. I guess they did the job correctly, since all of us that I know of made it!"

These lessons were not learned in thirty minutes or thirty days. They were life lessons learned over time. With patient assistants like Boots, Marvin and Marguerite gently guided three generations of young riders through a love affair with horses to become adults who could face any situation head on and know it could be tackled with "chin up and heels down."

The friends and family of Marvin and Marguerite were devastated to learn Monty would sacrifice his father's memory, character, and true spirit to gain the accolades of society and unimaginable wealth. They tried to understand him and failed. He refused to deal in reality or reason. Some thought he had lost his mind, and others wondered if he was on drugs. Perhaps the best answer came to Cheri Renebome Little in the middle of the night.

Throughout his life, Monty learned to win. He won everything. Perhaps the answer is buried, not in the grave with his parents, but in Monty's soul and the private hell in which he must live. For the one pair of boots he would never fill, the one man he could never best, the one loving and generous soul that Monty could not equal, was Marvin. Only by totally destroying his father, toppling a legend, could Monty find a final win.

A tragic loss was felt. The father's exceptional character was slain by the son's cruel word.

Monty's family begged him to retract only the statements about his father before his book was released in the United States. He refused. His stage had been set.

Marvin and Marguerite used to say there was a silver lining hiding in all the clouds of despair. From every loss, something is gained. From the loss of his parent's reputation, Monty gained fame and fortune. Monty contributes much to charity. Monty may live well from the fruit of *The Man Who Listens to Horses,* but he will also live the rest of his life with the knowledge of what he has done to earn it.

Likewise, if not for Monty's fame, *Horse Whispers & Lies* would not exist, the Red Pony Stall would not be dedicated to Marvin and Marguerite, and old friends would not have reunited.

On March 1, 1998, many contributors to this book met in Salinas at the Monterey County Sheriff's Posse Grounds to celebrate the lives of these two incredible humans. On that day, it was unanimously agreed that the truth needed to be told. Marvin and Marguerite deserved nothing less from those to whom they had dedicated their lives.

In Salinas, the house on Church Street is gone, but the beautiful magnolia stands. Fittingly, it shades the area just outside the John Steinbeck Library near the corner of Church and San Luis Streets. The Buena Vista Stables remains. Children still ride along the ever-changing banks of the Salinas River. The clapboard house still clings to a small patch of unyielding earth, and the echo of Marvin and Marguerite whispers softly through the cottonwoods not claimed by floods.

A dusty bottle of Chateau Napoleon, two California Horsemastership medallions, and a few silver belt buckles are at the back of an antique armoire, scarred and patched from a fifty-five-year-old bullet wound. In attics and closets, trophies and ribbons may be packed away . . . but the children remember.

Young riders continue to show at the Cow Palace, the posse grounds, and the big California Rodeo in Salinas. Marvin Roberts' hat hangs quietly in the museum at the rodeo grounds, and someday the interactive computer will tell the Roberts' story at the Red Pony Stall in the National Steinbeck Center.

Marvin and Marguerite never asked for much. They dreamed of a world where horses and children could enjoy one another. They did their best to bring joy to others, and to them, that brought happiness.

> "At its finest, rider and horse are joined not by tack, but by trust. Each is totally reliant upon the other. . . . Each is the selfless guardian of the other's very well-being."

—Michael J. Plumb

Truth Matters

The Man Who Listens to Horses was published as a nonfiction work and is entered in the Library of Congress as such. Without the refutation of *Horse Whispers & Lies*, Monty's book would forever be recounted as a factual historical record of the Roberts family.

Investigations show numerous discrepancies between fact and fiction that are not addressed in this book that is focused on the family.

To contribute to the **Red Pony Stall Exhibit at the National Steinbeck Center in Salinas,** write:

The National Steinbeck Center
In Memory of Marvin and Marguerite Roberts
One Main Street
Salinas, CA 93901

Regarding Monty and the mustang, *Shy Boy*, write:

U. S. Department of the Interior
Bureau of Land Management
Attn: Bureau Clearance Officer (WO-630)
1849 C Street, N.W.
Washington, DC 20240

If you believe readers of nonfiction have a right to trust a publisher, write:

Random House
Ms. Ann Godoff, President
201 East 50th Street
New York, NY 10022

and/or

Harper Collins
Ms. Jane Friedman
10 East 53rd Street
New York, NY 10022

A spokesperson from Random House said they no longer publish books by Monty Roberts. *Shy Boy*, Monty's latest book, was released by Harper Collins.

Ron Stolich, owner of Blooming Hills Thoroughbred Farms.

Larry Roberts and Suzanne Scott Koch.

Debra Ann Ristau and her mother, Joyce Martins Renebome, in 1999.

Lou Martins expresses sadness in 1998.

Ray Roberts and wife, Eleanor.

Joanne Church Taylor Johnson is responsible for the Red Pony Stall Exhibit dedication to Marvin and Marguerite.

Appendix I
Family Organization Chart

MONTY'S FAMILY MEMBERS IN *HORSE WHISPERS & LIES*

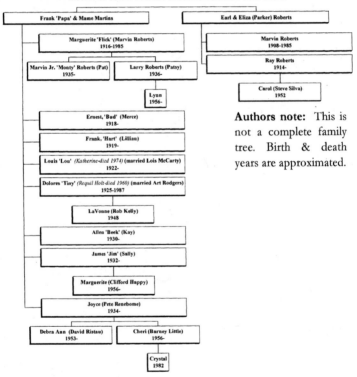

Frank 'Papa' & Mame Martins

Marguerite 'Flick' (Marvin Roberts)
1916-1985

Marvin Jr. 'Monty' Roberts (Pat)
1935-

Larry Roberts (Patsy)
1936-

Lynn
1956-

Ernest, 'Bud' (Merce)
1918-

Frank, 'Hart' (Lillian)
1919-

Louis 'Lou' *(Katherine-died 1974)* **(married Lois McCarty)**
1922-

Dolores 'Tiny' *(Requil Holt-died 1960)* **(married Art Rodgers)**
1925-1987

LaVonne (Rob Kelly)
1948

Allen 'Beek' (Kay)
1930-

James 'Jim' (Sally)
1932-

Marguerite (Clifford Happy)
1956-

Joyce (Pete Renebome)
1934-

Debra Ann (David Ristau)
1953-

Cheri (Barney Little)
1956-

Crystal
1982

Earl & Eliza (Parker) Roberts

Marvin Roberts
1908-1985

Ray Roberts
1914-

Carol (Steve Silva)
1952

Authors note: This is not a complete family tree. Birth & death years are approximated.

Appendix II

Joyce Martins Renebome

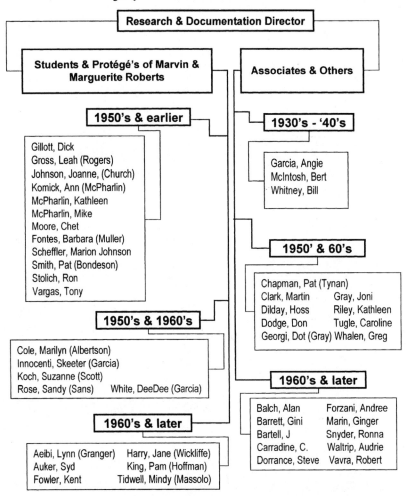

Research & Documentation Director

Students & Protégé's of Marvin & Marguerite Roberts

Associates & Others

1950's & earlier

Gillott, Dick
Gross, Leah (Rogers)
Johnson, Joanne, (Church)
Komick, Ann (McPharlin)
McPharlin, Kathleen
McPharlin, Mike
Moore, Chet
Fontes, Barbara (Muller)
Scheffler, Marion Johnson
Smith, Pat (Bondeson)
Stolich, Ron
Vargas, Tony

1930's - '40's

Garcia, Angie
McIntosh, Bert
Whitney, Bill

1950' & 60's

Chapman, Pat (Tynan)
Clark, Martin   Gray, Joni
Dilday, Hoss   Riley, Kathleen
Dodge, Don   Tugle, Caroline
Georgi, Dot (Gray)   Whalen, Greg

1950's & 1960's

Cole, Marilyn (Albertson)
Innocenti, Skeeter (Garcia)
Koch, Suzanne (Scott)
Rose, Sandy (Sans)   White, DeeDee (Garcia)

1960's & later

Balch, Alan   Forzani, Andree
Barrett, Gini   Marin, Ginger
Bartell, J   Snyder, Ronna
Carradine, C.   Waltrip, Audrie
Dorrance, Steve   Vavra, Robert

1960's & later

Aeibi, Lynn (Granger)   Harry, Jane (Wickliffe)
Auker, Syd   King, Pam (Hoffman)
Fowler, Kent   Tidwell, Mindy (Massolo)

A list of other significant contributors to *Horse Whispers & Lies*.
Our sincere apologies to anyone whose name was inadvertently omitted.

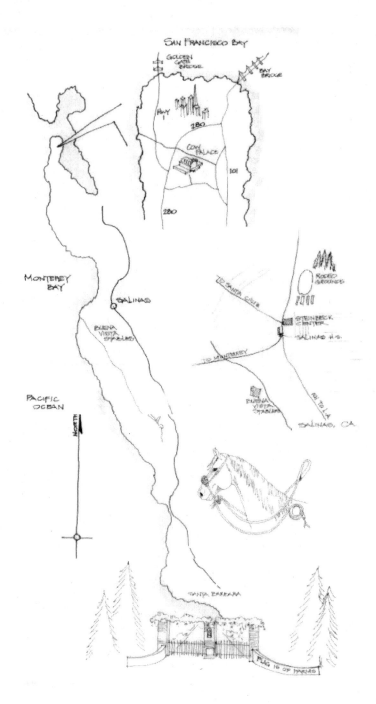

STEINBECK CENTER

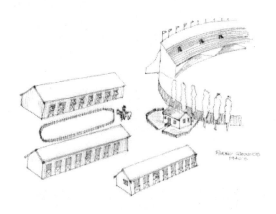

BUENA VISTA STABLES

Veracity Books was founded to publish books that embrace people and their passions with a focus on fact.

To order additional copies of *Horse Whispers & Lies,* write:

Veracity Books
PO Box 7010
Berkeley, CA 94707
Phone: (209) 543-0459 or (209) 744-1123
veracitybk@aol.com
http://www.horsewhispersandlies.com